Success at Any Age!

The Baby Boomer's and Gen Y Guide to becoming an Overnight Success

"creating businesses; creating jobs, and maintaining HOPE"

written and experienced by

Norm Bour

Published by BoomersSuccessGuide.com

Laguna Niguel, CA 92677
Copyright © 2012 Norm Bour
All rights reserved.

Cover design by Scott Herman

For large quantity sales, media interviews or speaking
engagement requests contact BoomersSuccessGuide.com
Written and printed in the United States of America
First edition published March, 2012

ISBN-13:
978-1470194673

Pre-release copy

Acknowledgments

This book has been three years in my mind, took ninety days to write and thirty years to experience. The difference between thinking about it and acting upon in it solely rests with Mike Brenhaug, who told me that I had the power to make this reality and offered advice and guidance that were critical to where I am today. A gentleman that went from an acquaintance to a friend to an Accountability Coach to a Mentor; I am forever indebted.

There were many that provided uplifting when I needed it and they did not even know they were doing it; it was just Who They Are. For all the positive spirits that I am surrounded by, I thank you and hope to return your positiveness and spirits of hope.

I have been blessed over the years to be surrounded by brilliant partners and friends that sometimes kept me from making a fool of myself and brought or kept me in line. Dave Naidu, one of the purest of hearts and brilliant man I have known, who brought me something I needed for 50 years- mentorship. Where the hell where you twenty years ago?!! My partners at Opis Network, some who have gone, and some who remain, like Michael Wedaa, who stepped up and offered a hand and allowed me the time I needed to complete my story.

Many favors were called in to bring this book to press and I thank all those that supported my efforts with generosity, heart and soul. Scott Herman and Gay Himebaugh and Raul Lozano (who has a heart much too big to contain!) for their kind "pay it forward" gestures. Also, based on one conversation, Dr. Shayne Tracy likewise paid it forward by giving me, gratis, the great web site that will be used to train and motivate and excite thousands of new businesses and many times more entrepreneurs.

A deep sense of love and appreciation to my cousin, Michael Tragarz, one of the most positive influences in my long life. When I shared my concept for The Guide, he offered nothing but support and encouragement, and some times that is the difference between failure and success. Sometimes you just need someone to believe in you when you question your own confidence.

Dedication

To my Mother, who never gave up on

me,

and to my wife, who finally did,

but stayed anyway.

Concepts, Ideas & People (AKA, table of contents)

Generational Overview: (dates vary)

People have a need to classify or categorize many things and one of the biggest identifiers that we focus on is "Which stage of life are we/ you in?" Going all the way back to the late 19th Century we gave each generation labels and called the immigrants from other countries specific names including the "New Worlders" and "Hard Timers", and later came the "Silent Generation" which were unfortunate to be born during our last Dark Economic Times; pre-World War II; our Great Depression babies, from 1925-1945. They were born in a good place at a bad time and you can be sure they are reflections of their times- good or bad- and their environment.

The **"Greatest Generation"** has been coined of those who fought in World War II and their significance and importance cannot be understated. During some of the most challenging times this nation ever encountered, the soldiers and citizens made the United States a *true* Super Power, a title we maintained for sixty plus years, but is becoming less and less secure as we are facing a Brand New World. One thing the Greatest Generation did with great fervor and with great success was have children; lots of them. And those children became the most significant demographical "movement" this nation has ever seen. So let's begin with them…

Baby Boomers: born 1946-1964 (Phase **III**)
They have been dissected to death since their numbers were so massive and influential for over half a century. Raised to think that job security was a reality, they have a

"take no prisoner" attitude, and were the first generation to buck the system en masse: Vietnam, drugs, liberal sex, disco, they exercised with focus, thought they could (and still do) live forever and not show their age. Peers include Bill Gates, Steven Jobs and other tech entrepreneurs. Most were raised with stay at home Moms, religion, the value of hard work and a "buck". Some have embraced the new technology and mastered it, and at the other extreme, some shun it completely. Due to less manual dexterity, vision challenges and mental focus, many Baby Boomers cannot multi-task nearly as well as the successive generations. Boomers do not see themselves as old! Even with graying (or no) hair and wrinkles, Boomers are still young on the inside!

The numbers: about 73 million.

Gen X: 1965-1980 (Phase **II**)

Children of Boomers: mostly working Moms, raised with divorce (about 40%), endured the last recessions of the 80's & 90's, energy crisis, the Berlin Wall crumbling and the earth flattening. Mostly raised with less bigotry, female power, higher education, many affluent parentage, AIDS crisis.

Sandwiched between 73 million Baby Boomers and 80 million Millennials, Generation X has just **46 million members**, making it a dark-horse demographic. Most of them are now approaching or in "Middle Age" which is a significant and sometimes precarious step in life. Questioning "what's it all about?" and "is this all there is?" can create many conflicts, both internally and externally. Loss and graying of hair, gaining of weight and loss of stamina can be treacherous to a healthy well-being and the realization that they are at "half-time" in the game can cause lots of angst. The proverbial "Middle Age Crazies" can cause many to come off their tracks, but it is also a time for reflection and giving back and becoming more aware of the "Big Picture" and the some times insignificance of the individual.

Gen Y: 1981-2000, (Phase **I**), AKA **Millennials**

Mostly under 30, also called the Echo Boomers since their numbers are larger than their parents: **about 80 million** strong. The Digital Generation: Raised with computers, many spoiled with a "everyone is wonderful" environment, uneasy in a "job" since they were not taught the value of hard work, but many are smart and try to craft shortcuts. Many leave home later, marry later, have kids later, or no kids, a bit selfish. Less religious, but more spiritual and even more color and race blind. Multicultural is the rule, not the exception. Absorbed with Smart Phones, Facebook, Twitter, Social Media and such, and comfortable with *less* personal, personal relationships, have short attention spans, like texting and instant messaging. They truly were BORN to multi-task and can work on homework, surf the web and listen to music with ear buds inserted all at the same time. And they can do them all reasonably well. They were raised with a world culture and enterprise and are used to world uncertainty and wars in distant lands.

They're young, smart, brash, wear flip-flops to work and listen to iPods at their desk. They want to work, but they don't want work to be their life. Gen Y doesn't take orders/ direction well, questioned their parents, and now they question their employers, don't take criticism well. They've been pampered, nurtured and programmed with activities since they were toddlers, and are considered "high-performance and high-maintenance" They also believe in their own worth.

• **Balance in their lives & jobs are important.** Unlike Boomers and the Generation before them, they are more interested in making their jobs accommodate their family and personal lives and want jobs with flexibility, telecommuting options and the ability to work part-time, shared-time or leave the job to accommodate kids. After 9/11 they grew to the realization that life is short and they value it more.

• **Change, change, and more change.** They don't expect to stay in a job, or even a career, for too long and will have many over the course of their lives, and they're skeptical of Big Business and employee loyalty. They don't like to stay any one place too long and are a generation that multi-task with ease. "They're like Generation X on steroids," says Bruce Tulgan of Rainmaker Thinking from New Haven, Connecticut.

Introduction: How it all began:

Success can come at any age and though no one is ever *born* successful, many die that way. "How do you define success?" Is it measured in dollars and cents? There are many that die wealthy but consider themselves failures. Does it mean helping many along the way? Is it saving a dog, a child, or the world? There is no one answer and everyone defines it their own way. The more important question is WHEN did success occur? What prompted the "I feel successful" mindset?

There may be parts of this book that may seem rather "heavy" but they really need to be shared. The goal is to assure you that the struggles and the challenges you face- and will face- can be endured and all obstacles can be overcome. "You may lose confidence, but never lose hope," is a credo I live with, so bear with me as I share the failures I've worked through to finally come to the realization that "failures are temporary; success is a state of mind."

If you are a Gen Y reader, take these words to heart. Everyone comes from some place and I was in your shoes and looked at life with much clearer eyes in my twenties, just like you. If I can help you avoid some of the challenges you are sure to face and increase the speed of your success path, then we both win.

This book could save your life; it could save mine. That may sound dramatic, but imagine being a man of 57 that is going through his second bankruptcy and about to lose his house and wife of 25 years and everything that was held dear for over two decades? The story sadly is true and the number of times I have thought about giving up are too many to count. How about you? Have you also given up or thought about quitting? After 25, 30, or more years of busting your ass and still not getting "there", why continue? I have asked myself that question as I am sure you have too. So here's the thing. Achieving "success" has many different facets and definitions. How do you define it?

Sorry this book is so late…

I meant to write this book before I hit age 55. There were so many things coming into place and I just knew that after decades of trying it was finally time to have *my* ship come in. Sometimes things don't work out as planned. As I was finally writing this long overdue cathartic treatise I found my very first, original draft from November 23, 2008, which was over three years ago. The idea already was in my mind, but I put it aside. It wasn't till years later that I realized that I was not getting any younger, shit happens, and if I was going to leave anything behind, I hoped it would be something positive; something hopeful.

So here it is, a few years later, and even though my ship has not arrived yet, maybe this book will inspire, teach or motivate you to keep trying. Speaking for myself I came close to giving up. Discouragement is unavoidable and it's easy to get frustrated when things don't pan out. There were dark mental stages when I wondered why I kept striving when it was oh, so easy to not. I considered suicide more than once and two of my business partners had close friends that did just that. They lost their fortunes or their jobs and killed themselves. That state of mind is a horrible one, so if you have thought about such crap, get that lunacy out of there. What is especially sad is that there are many "young people" out there that likewise have or have had these dark thoughts. Purge them, please.

Being the only son of a concentration camp survivor pretty much makes failure or giving up not an option. If my Mother could spend four years at Auschwitz and walk out of there skinny and shaken and go on living with that for 67 more years, then how could failure in business be any worse? So even though this book is not about me, I do think it's important to understand where I came from.

My biological father was pretty much a non-entity in my life. If you think of the term "sperm-donor" that fits his description. He was not a bad or mean person, but when he met my mother in 1953, and she had been out of a concentration camp for less than ten years, what he saw was a housekeeper and someone to cook for him and cater to his needs. He wasn't a drunk or anything like that, he just wasn't "present" in their relationship nor was he in mine. It wasn't until I was in my fifties that I found something out about their marriage that literally made me speechless. As my Mom was in her advanced years (she died peacefully at age 90) we started getting even closer since she needed my guidance and love and I knew our years/ days were numbered. So one day we're talking about Dad and what kind of relationship they had and she said to me, "I never told you this, but we only had sex *one time*." Now I knew my Father was not a passionate man and I knew I was conceived prior to their wedding, (unless I was the only 7-month full gestation baby), but them having sex just once and bearing me was a Shock to the System. My Father just didn't have much of a drive for sex or anything for that matter. Another important detail to bring up is that I am an only child, which is not that unusual, but the reasons are. Mom remarried but had no more children, and she always called me her "Miracle Baby." Not to discount any Mother's love for their children, but my Mother was way over the top because family was important to her, especially as she watched her Mother and younger sister walk to their deaths at the Auschwitz Concentration Camp.

Her experience in the Camp was something that haunted her her entire life and had a deep impact on me. She was one of the first prisoners in Auschwitz and was not freed until the end of the war. In that Hell she saw things we could not imagine and experienced things that we couldn't either. The German doctors were infamous for performing medical experiments on the Jews, some more extreme than others, and my Mother was likewise victimized, but the one that had the deepest impact, the most severe was the doctors performing on her a hysterectomy; the removal of the uterus, or womb. Theoretically by removing that organ there is no way for a woman to carry a child to birth, yet here I am. The efficiency of German doctors was less than German-like and many things they did were on a massive scale, including Jewish sterilization. Some doctors were more competent than others and many surgeries were botched, including this one. The irony is that my Mom's operation was performed by one of their medical leaders-THE medical leader- Dr. Josef Mengele, also known as the Angel of Death, since much of the horror was orchestrated under his direction.

In 1943 he took over active day to day operations of the medical experiments at Auschwitz and continued to do so for over a year until the camp was closed and the war over. Prior to that, he was self-honored by calling himself the "Decider of Fates" and directed those that came off the cattle trains to one of two lines. One line- the healthy line- was deemed able to work, and the other was where the old, frail, too young or otherwise impaired were sent directly to the gas chamber. He wore a white doctor's smock and with his hands raised like a Messiah he evoked sheer power to control life and death which is how he was bestowed the name "Angel of Death." It was this man, with my Mother watching, that sent my maternal grandmother to her death, holding the hand of my Mother's little sister, my Aunt to never be. Some time later as her older sister was brought to the Camp she was able to exert some influence to actually save her life, but that story will be saved for another time.

Though Mengele's tenure in Auschwitz was brief and his time as an active butcher was even more brief, my Mother was one of his unlucky patients. In addition to the love she gave me she also willed me something just as powerful which took me years to realize, and that was the Will to Survive. Though I have been fortunate to not have to fight for my life or be in any life-threatening situations, her experiences and her determination to live through what she endured was subconsciously imprinted in my psyche. So when I face failure after failure and just want to give it all up-- I can't. It would dishonor all she lived through and the legacy that she left behind in me and in others. If you think that Rose's experiences left her with scars you are 100% correct. Born in Hungary in 1919, the middle daughter of a man that abandoned his family, raised in what we would call a ghetto or slum with her siblings, mother and grandparents and then having to live though her horror? Even though she was the biggest worrier and pessimist in the world, I could not fault her for it, even though I did. Her extreme experience actually caused me to sway to the opposite pole as an extreme optimist, so her legacy lives on through me and I have to appreciate that.

We reach certain points in our lives and wonder "Is this all there is?" Money does not buy happiness, that is for sure, but we'll focus on those that have reached financial success, regardless of how they defined it. Many people at any stage of their lives can consider themselves to be "successful" and for the most part they are right. It is a state of mind and many have been broke, but happy and considered their journey satisfying. For others they may be rich beyond the realm of most people yet they still consider themselves failures. How many celebrities have killed themselves either overtly or by lifestyle until they finally succumb? The most recent example: Whitney Houston.

So regardless of which generational phase you are in you will learn how others have done it and possibly apply their lessons and experiences to your own life. Speaking for myself, as I approach "retirement age" which is an elusive term at best, I personally find success to be one where I reach a State of Peace where I work doing what I want, working as much or as little as I want and finding satisfaction towards whatever peace I want in my life. How about you? What are your goals? This book is about your dreams, fulfilled or not and the dreams yet to be realized. If what follows motivates you to keep trying and not give up, then it is worth every minute it took me to get here.

Finding success early- or not...

Many reach that Successful State of Mind at an amazingly early age and in today's high tech world it is actually easier to reach earlier than ever before. When I was young the cliché was "I want to be a millionaire by the time I am 30." That age was an arbitrary benchmark in most young persons' minds that signified that they/ we/ I are approaching the "maturation stage." That is BS of course and some mature much earlier than that and others never do- at any age! No matter now much money I made, it was never enough and it seems my whole life I was trying to capture that Brass Ring that was just out of my grasp.

When I was 23 I moved to Southern California and got a job at a car dealership in the service department. I had similar jobs at other dealerships so I knew it well and was good at it. My starting salary was $1200 per month which at that time was OK wages, but not significant. My overhead was low, I had no car payment and rent was affordable. I always wanted more and said inside my head, "If I could just make $1500 per month I'd really be set." And sure enough as I got better at my job I started making that income and you know what? It wasn't enough. It afforded me the ability to get a better car, a used one, and that extra expense wiped out the added income. So now my internal mind said, "If I could just make $2,000 per month I'd be good." And of course I made it and $2,000 was better, but it was not good enough. Like many of you I had that same internal conversation my entire career and as much as I made it was never enough for very long. It wasn't until recently that I gave up. I gave up trying to control everything and everyone. I gave up trying to create a business with clients that had no interest. I gave up trying to maintain a marriage that had long run its course. And I gave up in just one day; the last day of 2011, and it was like a Reawakening. All the pressure, all the stress and everything that weighed me down was released with one conversation. Of course there was a build up to get to that point, but the pressure valve of my life was let go. This probably sounds like an exaggeration, but this transformation literally created a brand new me. I focused on the book—this book-- and before you know it other amazing opportunities came into my world. Totally out of the blue and totally outside my comfort zone, but that's OK. I gave in, if you will, to accepting things I wasn't looking for and the peace of mind and sense of freedom has been life altering. One of my business partners had a saying: *"When you give up control of your business, you regain control of your life."* I didn't really understand that until it happened.

You'll find as we continue this journey that others have gone through similar processes and have had similar outcomes. For the Boomers that have struggled for years putting that square peg in the round hole I hope that maybe these case studies will encourage you to find a knife and whittle that square peg into a more well-rounded one. The result is that you will be better-rounded too. Don't wait. The questions I want you to ask yourself are "Why not here? Why not now? Why not *me*?" For three years this book idea was isolated into a back corner of my mind. Every once in a while I opened that door and looked into that corner but never did anything about it. I always had an unbridled sense of optimism and mostly disappointed myself, and many times other people, so I was scared. I had never undertaken a project of this magnitude before and it wasn't until I realized that I needed to get it out that I finally summoned the courage to do it and complete it.

I did it for me, but I did it for you, too. If you've had Dark Thoughts that made you question yourself and wonder if it was all worth it and if you could still continue, then consider this moment in time a resting point. Take a pause, take a breath and let go of your doubts, or at least trying to control them. See what others have gone through; learn what I have gone through and if you get just one nugget of inspiration and hope, then this journey makes it all worthwhile. Success is a state of mind, so by all means define it in your own terms.

How do you define success? Is it just about business? Financial and money? Life and relations? Accomplishments in your chosen career and path? It is a personal choice and everyone will reach their own conclusion.

You will find that most of the people whose stories I share started their businesses from scratch. Not a one of them bought a business or a franchise. These were self-starting enterprises that began because they were laid off. Or because they saw a need. Or because they wanted more control of their lives. Or because they were inspired?

The term Gen Y (Phase I), Gen X (Phase II) and Baby Boomers (Phase III) are already defined, but there are also some unique characteristics to each:
1. With Phase I success *there are no rules.*
2. Phase II, hitting it big between ages 30-50, is usually the "sweet spot."
3. With Phase III, experience counts tremendously and can overcome overwhelming odds. You can offset and compensate for lower energy with higher motivation and clearer focus.

4. Phase I Millennials are open minded, do what they want- preferably if it's COOL- and they have nothing to lose. They are invincible, they are not cynical or damaged and they have plenty of time to recover if they fail. And for the most part they are correct.

5. Phase II is driven more by money and a sense of accomplishment; they usually have a family and must support them, make them proud, yet still find time to spend with them. They have some experience (and failures) under their belts so feel they are better equipped to become successful. They still have plenty of time but as they approach 50 they understand that failure is more difficult to repair.

6. The Boomers, Phase III, are driven by money and because they HAVE TO. There is little time to recover and as they face retirement, mortality and the lack of a legacy they are high in motivation.

So with all that said, let's take our first step

(1) Gen Y success: achieving success before age 30; *there are no rules*

I cannot speak for you so I can only share my personal experiences and those of the persons profiled in this book. Achieving success before age 30 is not nearly as difficult as it was 20, 30 or more years ago. And yes, that may sound like and be an excuse for why I have not done it, but even so there are three main reasons: knowledge, information, and technology.

Growing up in the 70's, education was a commodity that was nice to have, but not critical. Pre computers, much of what was taught were the same basics that had been taught for the previous two decades. The economy surely changed, and world powers changed, and the world started to move much quicker. A college education forty years ago, which could be had for about $10,000 for a four-year degree, was an absolute door opener when it came to getting a job after graduation and to begin a career path. For those without an education it was hit or miss and the career path either came to us and we stayed with it, or we had to make our own determination of what career we did want. And one not *requiring* a degree. During those days you could almost compete without a degree if you had skills, personality, possibly some connections and the drive to go after what you want.

That lack of a degree could be made up by something that college does not necessarily supply, and that is knowledge; applied knowledge; street smarts, and the general tag for that is called "information." In today's world information has never been so accessible, whether it comes from the Internet or the Smart Phone, or from the fact that there are no limitations to learn about anything and everything you need to plod your life's journey. During the 1970's information was getting a little easier to find since computers were becoming more commonplace and data was more accessible. That's where technology starts making success at an earlier age so much more practical and available.

Thirty years ago there were certain "paths" that made success easier than just blind hope and wandering. Many started a business or bought a business or took over a family business and those three vehicles have just as much potential and power today than it ever did. You rarely or ever heard of someone as a teen starting a business and later selling it for millions of dollars! That just did not happen. Many teens started a paper route, landscaping or gardening business or some blue collar trade that took more manpower than intellect, but teen superstars were a rare commodity. Television, movies and music did bring some of these young adults to the forefront, but today and with the Internet, someone with just a bit of talent and a lot of ambition and tech savvy can become an overnight sensation. Just ask Justin Bieber or Rebecca Black who wrote a song called "Friday" which became a Youtube sensation- and embarrassment- but after several weeks it went viral and got over 30M hits. It garnered her an appearance on Late Night TV and currently her song is being used by Kohl's department store for their holiday shopping jingle. Did she do this as a lark? To make money? Probably a bit of both, but at age fourteen her path probably did not happen by design and where it goes from here is anyone's guess.

My twenties were full of promise. After goofing off until age 26 I finally got serious and got my real estate license and practiced my craft in Orange County, California. When I started in 1981 the Prime rate was 20.5% and the realtors that went through the Boom Years of the late seventies were crying the blues. The market was suddenly TOUGH and doing business was HARD! But sales were made and it took creativity to make them happen. Prices were low (by today's standards) and the job market was respectable, though not booming. These were the days when you could officially "take over" or assume a mortgage, so even though new loan rates were high, the older loans in the single digits were the Golden Goose. If ever there was a heyday for "creative financing" in residential real estate it was the early eighties! Computer tracking by lenders and regulators was very weak and buyers and sellers were creating their own mortgages and seller financing and in addition to the first mortgage on most homes, sometimes there were two, three, four and even up to FIVE loans against a property.

Being a rookie I did as I was told. My broker says "hold open house", I did it. He says "make cold calls", I (grudgingly) did that too. Knock on doors; walk the neighborhood, the market required that we did whatever it took to make it work. And in my twenties I had energy and motivation and dreams and goals and I KNEW that by the time I was thirty the market would "recover" and I would be a millionaire. Really. That was my goal and I wrote it down and did all the Positive Affirmations, but I guess the Keys to the Kingdom were not due me yet.

I also got involved with the field of Financial Planning since I saw so many people that made really good money yet had nothing for a down payment at all. Some things never change. I studied for my Certified Financial Planner (CFP) test and got my Series 7 Securities license, the most difficult to get, and was ready to control not just one profession, but two. I never completed my CFP classes and stopped at level five in a six part series. WHY? Because the real estate market, after years of malaise, was finally showing signs of life and in the mid-eighties we had the first Real Estate Boom of my (then) young life. The stock market on October 19, 1987 took a nosedive and dropped 22% in ONE DAY and billions of dollars were lost and suddenly people become gun-shy of the stock market and they wanted to put their money in hard assets: real estate. And this crash was one of the first that was actually a GLOBAL event and affected 19 of the top 20 markets worldwide and saw them all drop 20% or more in a single day. Computer and Program Trading showed their dark sides which resulted in changes in the years to come. The real estate market had actually started to show signs of life for a year or so prior to this event, but this was the catalyst that triggered a massive shift. It was challenging and I started making good-not great- money and lived comfortably, but never came close to being a millionaire or ever feeling that I "made it." In our twenties we are way too focused on money some times. Many of the people I interviewed for this story were much smarter and they DID make it before they hit 30, and I saw that by tapping into available resources it was easier to do than ever before.

The Under 30 crowd today has more potential and opportunities than ever. A great web site called www.under30CEO.com is a good example of specifically focused and dedicated support networks to sustain and engage young entrepreneurs. A young man name Louis Lautman actually created a film and an organization called Young Entrepreneur Society (YES) which again, supports young entrepreneurs and he created a movie called "The YES Movie" which profiles dozens of successful youth business persons, including some under age 10!

So what drives a young Gen Y and how are they different from a Phase III seasoned vet? The Millennials are driven by an unbridled optimism and a sense of having no fear or nothing to lose. Plus it is cool to make more money than your parents before you hit puberty or teen-hood!

I interviewed dozen of persons under age 30 that hit what they call (and I agree) "financial success" and "made it" and their stories are all different, but there are common themes:

- Most of them are self-employed. It is very difficult to "make it" as an employee of any company by the Third Decade.
- Surprisingly many of these business models are very low tech or no-tech at all. Many times we think that most under-thirty success stories are the whiz kids that develop software or write an on-line game and hit it big based on brainpower, but none in that class are included here. This qualifier is *especially* significant since it means that these ideas are available to anyone *at any age*.
- Some of them come from "successful" parentage, and I only define that as those with parents that are supportive or entrepreneurial in their own right or ones that encouraged their kids to attend college or further their education. Which brings up another contradictory revelation:
- Most of them are not college graduates, yet some have advanced degrees. The point is that a college degree is not necessary in many fields, critical in others, and nice to have in most. So if you never got yours or think it's too late, what is stopping you from getting it or finding alternatives? Just don't planning on getting a J-O-B in that field if you are a Boomer or over the age of 50.

(2) Phase II success: hitting it big between ages 30-50; the "sweet spot"

The chances to become financially independent or even comfortable while in your twenties are still a long shot. After college, which eats into at least 2-3 years of this decade, you now have just half a dozen more to fast-track your career or come up with a Winning Business Model. The twenties are a time for maturing; exploration, failure, and picking yourself up and doing what needs to be done.

The years from 30-50 are what I call the Sweet Spot, since this is when life settles into some type of system or pattern that you can now build upon. Whether you start your own business, buy one or inherit one, these are the years to try new things since the open-minded, no failure mindset remains in full force. If you are an employee of a company these are the years to "climb the ladder" to coin an over-used expression, but it really is true. If you are single you have no ties to stop you from moving from one fair opportunity to another great one. If you are with a great company with room for growth, you can move wherever in the world you want to go. And I encourage anyone reading this to do just that, regardless of your financial position or gender. Today's world offers opportunities for anyone that wants to take those risks. If you are married, options still remain as long as you have a supportive spouse, and even with children that should not be an excuse to not reach the goals you set for yourself.

The time of life between ages 30-50 is a grand one and after going through it I sometimes did not appreciate it as much as I should have. During our twenties we are ruled by emotions and hormones and a little bit (or a lot) of rebellion that makes it so exciting. Failure is typically not an option and many feel invulnerable. In your twenties you can (usually) eat- and drink- what you want and your fast-paced metabolism will burn it away. Thrill sports abound and are worth trying. For me I went skydiving, hang gliding, did some mountain climbing, snow skied a lot and got into motorcycles. Also did some martial arts but I found most of these experiments did not "stick" very long. You either have an internal drive to pursue them or you don't. There was really only one thing that got and kept me excited and that was the world of business. Unfortunately I had no degree and my excitement and motivation both outweighed by talents and skills and I ended up failing far more that I won. I got a reputation for trying "everything" as some might put it, but I had no sense of failure. The future was wide open and with a bit of knowledge under my belt from my Roaring Twenties I was fearless.

Reality came into play in my early thirties when I broke my first bone. Ever. I was very lucky as a child and teen and had amazing resiliency when it came to injuries. I had fallen many times and always walked away uninjured. Time and metabolism- and de-calcification- takes its toll and as we age our bodies do not recover as quickly. After my first major ski fall, breaking my right shoulder and left wrist at the same time, I realized that maybe it was time to cool my jets a bit. I took the next winter off and two years later I hit the slopes again, full of insight and vigor and again feeling indestructible. Another bad fall at a local ski resort and this time breaking my OTHER, left side shoulder convinced me to give up the sport. And I had to promise my wife since she was the one that saw me come home in a sling twice in three years.

The way I felt about skiing was the way I felt about business. I became a licensed Realtor when I was 26 and thought I could take on the world. After just a few years I lost my "love" for the business, but continued on for about 15 more, all the while trying new things. Multi-level companies showed great promise so I tried more than I care to admit, buying thousands of dollars of products and even going so far as to produce an infomercial for some of my products. Twice! All failed but that did not bother me and I kept on keeping on. At the time the word "entrepreneur" was not as common-place as it is today, but that is what I was. I really wasn't aware, all the more reason that today it is marginally easier to DEFINE who and what you are, find others like you and develop peer to peer counseling to advance your cause. Being tagged "Entrepreneur" is more than just a title, label or tag; it is a state of mind, one that we will explore shortly.

In my forties I got a bit smarter, looked for and thought I found something I was lacking- a mentor- and got into some real business opportunities. And failed miserably, to the point of filing for bankruptcy protection. You see the mentor I thought I had found was a borderline criminal and psychopath, but I drank his Kool Aid. Sometimes when you have so much drive and ambition you may follow false leads or prophets, so be warned and be smart. To say that I had lost confidence in myself and had lost some respect from my family is mostly true and it got to the point where I had to do something I was not looking forward to: getting a job.

In all my 5½ decades I have had just a few actual j-o-b-s and I was a bad employee. Always looking for things to do better and different and trying to think outside the box made me more rebellious than many employers wanted to deal with. The years I spent in real estate and my experiments in entrepreneurship and the experience of going through the credit issues and bankruptcy made me highly qualified to move into my next life cycle- the world of mortgages. Starting as an employee and being highly productive and making a lot of money put me in the best Sweet Spot I had been in for years. I thought (mistakenly) that being an employee offered some degree of job security but found that to be false. The company where I worked went through an internal change with new management and attitude and shrunk from a company of 125 or so employees to less than ten, all in a six-month period. I was one of the ten that remained as long as I could, but recognized a sinking ship. But that experience did teach me enough to consider opening my own mortgage company and that is what I did, and quite successfully until the crash during the first decade of the New Millennium.

Enough about me, so back to your thirties to fifties window. What I described may be similar to what you have experienced or maybe not. If you are younger than 30 you may grin at the pompousness of going through all that, but the point is, this time period is ripe with opportunities. So try not to blow it like I did.

(3) Boomer success: hitting it big after Age 50

So imagine this- and for some it may not be difficult at all. You're in your fifties. You've worked hard all your life, even worked smartly, or so you think. You've done OK, bought new cars over the years, probably a home or two; possibly invested in rental property, the stock market or any number of way too many options available on which to spend your money. You've probably had kids which may or may not be gone from the house, maybe even still worrying about expensive college expenses in case you got a late start. You may be an employee of a company, probably not for too many years; longevity and security in any company is getting increasingly rare. At one time the average person by they time they reach "retirement age", say 65-70, would have gone through three, maybe four different careers. Now according to the Bureau of Labor Statistics and echoed by many academics you may be looking at seven. Personally I think for most of the Gen Xs and Gen Ys it may be more. The reality of today is not the reality of the way the world used to be until the 1980's. The concept of starting a career in your twenties and staying with the same company and retiring there forty years later is like a fairy tale from years gone by.

If you weren't an employee and you were self-employed in any sense of the word, your experience over the past decades may have been much different. Whether you owned a restaurant or retail shop; were in a "professional" field like medicine, law, real estate, insurance, banking or any one of dozens of others, or if you were a tradesperson with your own plumbing business, electrical, automotive, or again, one of several dozen or more to choose from; the reality is *your business is NOT like it once was*. And it may never be again. The economic downturn has affected most every business owner and unless you are in the "damage control" or damage repair business, like credit repair, or bankruptcy business, most every one of you has seen your business drop from a single digit reduction to upwards of 20% or more.

Again, back to reality. If you are in your fifties and you have not "made it", whether as an employee or self-employed, you are not alone. Even if you thought you had it made, that rug may have been removed by the economy with its double digit lay offs of millions of employees and the general downturn of not just the national economy, but the worldwide meltdown as well. The reality is, virtually no one has escaped unscathed and nearly everyone has been affected in some way. The pension plan, IRA, or 401K plans you thought would carry into your Golden Years are probably a fragment of what they were during the peak.

So, all those years of striving and trying and struggling and you still haven't "made it" yet? Welcome to the Way Too Crowded Club and one where the initiation costs are lost opportunities and misgivings over roads not taken.

Now it's time to share my "great reveal"; the motivation for writing this book. It is not too late and it is not time to despair. It is time to look at yourself honestly and candidly and find your strengths- capitalize on them- and remove or repair your weaknesses. Can you really be an "overnight success" after 25 years of trying? You can if you think you can. If you think it's too late, you may be correct, too.

We talked about the motivators in the worlds of Phases I and II. The Gen Ys are full of unbridled optimism, energy; a can-do attitude along with a failure is not an option mindset. They have energy and the one thing that NONE of the Boomers will ever have again: **Time**. Time runs out for all of us and the Millennials don't even have that concept in their mind. The middle phase is also blessed with time, and comforted and fine tuned with and by experience. They are motivated to make up for lost time in many cases and when they start looking at their lives as a time line and see that there may be more time BEHIND THEM than IN FRONT, they start sensing their mortality. Failure IS an option since in many cases they have had it before. Now the unbridled optimism is tempered by a sense of reality in that it IS possible- even likely- to fail in any venture. Boomers are in Phase III and have a 'Take No Prisoners' mindset; they (we) *cannot, must not* lose. The money we lose in any given venture in many cases cannot be recovered. The *time* we lose is lost forever. And the reality check of seeing your life as 2/3 over or more creates a sense of despair and fear. And rightfully so. Our best health years are usually behind us, along with waning energy levels and moments of enthusiasm. To *keep that* level of positiveness IS an effort and must be done intentionally and internally, and it will probably not happen unless you make it happen.

My goal is not just to plant that seed and walk away and say "now do it." The plan is to learn from the Millennials and Gen Xs and especially those Boomers that HAVE made it in their later years. The good news is that if you don't have a college degree right now you probably won't need one. If you do have one, it probably won't matter and you can take your resume and put it aside. If you really want to "make it" you will probably have to do it on your own- which *does not necessarily mean by yourself*. It is easy to fail alone, but hard to succeed alone. What it means is that the likelihood of getting a J-O-B and developing a career at this point and "making it" is highly unlikely. Face it. It's time to find the entrepreneur inside or develop and hone the talents you have into something that can make you some money. Others have done it and are doing it right now. The economy we are living in is absolutely the most *level playing field* in our long lives. You or anyone can compete with the "Big Boys" and with technology and the Internet you can be anywhere in the world doing your thing and seem like you are right next door. We have all been experiencing the "Flat World" over the past 25 years, so now it's time to use that to your advantage, just as many have before. You probably do not NEED a lot of money, but you may have to tap into your rainy day fund or money you thought would take you into those Golden Years. Going into those years broke and despondent is not my intention and I would like to encourage you to work to avoid that at all costs. This is where we are going, the journey I wish you all to take. Hope you are ready.

"Do, or do not. There is no 'try."
Master Yoda

(4) Others have also been late to the party...

In Phase III we sometimes think our lives are over and it is too late. For many that will be the case and there are some things that you just cannot do any more. Your "Days in the Sun", "Glory Days" or whatever rock song resonates with you have passed and you will no longer be a professional baseball player (or sports figure of any type, unless it's passive, like poker); you will probably not be a Rock Star, not withstanding the huge list of those in their sixties and seventies and damn close to their eighties that are still pulling it off. Yes, Tony Bennett is 85 years old as I write this, but even the Eveready Rabbit will eventually run out of juice.

Even with that said there are many famous and non-famous people that did not hit the Big Time till they were over 50. And many of them find and found success in very distinctive ways, including _**writing**_ and the _**arts**_. The good thing about aging is that our bodies may not be as strong as they once were, but in many cases our minds are sharp. Let's review some patterns for what we now term the Phase III successes.

Mr. "Kentucky Fried Chicken", Colonel Harlan Sanders: the consummate Entrepreneur

The first person that comes to many persons' minds is Colonel Sanders. Harland Sanders was no slouch as a young man, but he didn't become the bow-tied chicken mogul success we know and love until he was **65**. And to get facts clear, he never was a Colonel. That title was an honorary one given many Southern Gents by the Governor of Kentucky, the Honorable Order of Kentucky Colonels.

He worked on the railroad as a young man and always had determination and will, later entering college and becoming an attorney. Since these were the Henry Ford, "car in every garage" days, one thing that Harlan noticed was the explosive growth of automobiles. Still coming out of the horse & buggie days this was a shock and he saw the potential for profit. Living in a rural area of Kentucky he also saw lots of cars and the growing need for gas and gas stations to fill them, so that is where he put his money and bought a station. He wasn't the only one that saw potential and there was more competition than he cared to see, so he put his innovation hat on and sought ways to stand out; to be distinctive.

In addition to the automobile drivers he also shared many conversations with the long-distance haulers and truckers and those traversing up and down the eastern coast. and many of them had the same complaint: the lack of quality food on the road. Trying to keep things simple he added a sitting area to his gas station and offered just three types of food: ham, roast beef and fried chicken. It didn't take long for him to realize the chicken was the draw and in short order he had patrons visiting his establishment for the food more than the gas. And to help keep them longer he added a motel, going so far as to create a 100% accurate motel room adjoining the restaurant and placing the rest room IN the motel room. Since most motels at that time were seedy, run down affairs, his pristine and clean room kept his travelers longer than some had planned. As others saw how successful that made him they also tried to play the game of one upmanship and Harlan went to the kitchen trying to craft the perfect chicken recipe. By this time he was over 40 years old.

Over the following years he tried many combinations, trying to find the "perfect" blend. "Dad drove us crazy," his daughter Margaret complained, "but when he finally found the perfect combination of 11 herbs and spices and cooked just the right way in his pressure cooker (as opposed to a frying pan) he finally stayed with perfection." The pressure cooker was more than for just taste, but also decreased the cooking time for his chicken by more than 50%. His recipe soon caught the attention of everyone but it took another twenty years plus before he opened his first Kentucky Fried Chicken franchise. The bucket, and the slogan, "finger lickin' good" were his concepts and he become a celebrity icon throughout the South. His rise to fame as owner was just over 10 years, but being the marketing genius he was, he made the most of it. His trademark white suit, cane and handlebar mustache made him everyone's favorite grandfather and when he sold his interest, he stayed on as a pitchman.

Before his ship came in he came very close to losing everything when the Interstate Highway bypassed his little goldmine. We think it's a Hollywood fabrication when we hear of rural towns that were decimated when the interstate bypass sent the cars traveling by at 60 miles per hour, but the Colonel was so victimized. He sold his motel, restaurant and station for a fraction of their former value and was near destitute at age 66, living off social security and some savings. Even though he lost his building and business he kept his pressure cooker and recipe and traveled throughout the country selling his recipes and later his franchises and in just four years he had over 400 locations nationwide and sold the whole enterprise for just $2 million to a group of investors. He stayed on as spokesman and traveled endlessly and got an annual salary of $40,000.

The company later went public and was purchased by the conglomerate Heublein and the Colonel got no part of it.

He passed away at age 90 and just a few years after the company was sold again to PepsiCo for $840 million.

Laura Ingalls Wilder: writer

"Little House on the Prairie" is an iconic book series which became a very popular television show in the seventies and eighties. The author, Laura Wilder, spent most of her life as a farmer's wife and early on was a teacher and actually lived the prairie lifestyle she wrote about. Born in 1867 in rural Wisconsin, she was one of five children and wrote about what she knew and even though she was a writer for decades she did not "hit the big time" until she published her first novel. At **65** years old.

She was prompted by her daughter who was becoming a writer of notoriety so Laura became a columnist in her mid 40's. It wasn't until twenty years later that she became the prolific- and well paid writer- that she turned out to be and continued her writing into her later years, almost until she died at age 90.

There is a lesson to be learned. If you've had the urge to write, just do it, regardless of your age. Write about what you know, or take the wisdom of the decades and spin a yarn that will engage the readers.

Taikichiro Mori: real estate tycoon

You don't have to start early to become the richest man in the world. Mori was an economics professor until he left academia at age **55** to become a real estate investor in 1959. Mori had recently inherited a couple of buildings from his father, and he jumped headfirst into Tokyo's real estate scene.

Mori started his second career by investing in the Minato ward where he spent his childhood, and within a matter of years he was presiding over Japan's real estate boom. He had a knack of developing personal relationships and trust with many of his tenants and his company, Mori Building Company thrived for decades.

When Mori died in 1993, he was Forbes' two-time reigning world's richest man with a net worth of around $13 billion and over $3B ahead of his rival. Soon he would be eclipsed by a rising and wealthier star in Seattle, Bill Gates. Even so, he was something of a Japanese precursor to Warren Buffett, and like Buffett never seemed totally comfortable with the fame and fortune his second career won him. If you saw him in the street you would never know that he was so blessed and always lived a fairly modest life. Even in researching him there is not as much public information as many with a fraction of his wealth.

Grandma Moses: painter

Anna Mary Robertson Moses is one of the biggest names in American folk art, and she didn't even pick up a brush until after she was 80 years old. As we will see throughout this book, the creatives in many cases do not flourish until their later years.

Grandma Moses was originally a big fan of embroidery, but once her arthritis grew too painful for her to hold a needle, and guided by suggestions from her sister, she decided to try painting.

She was **76** when she cranked out her first canvas, and she lived another 25 years as a painter -- long enough to see the canvases she had sold for $3 sell for more than $10,000. It was at age 78 that a New York engineer and art collector bought her pieces on display in a drug store window for just $3.00-$5.00, liked what he saw, and went to her home to purchase ten more. A year later they were on display at the Museum of Modern Art and were a great hit and pushed prices upwards.

Her Folk Oriented, down home paintings were enjoyed by the public and ended up on Christmas cards, fabric and unusual mediums of all types. Just ten years after that collector bought her paintings for peanuts she was honored by President Truman at the White House. Like many artists in history, some are worth more dead than alive, but she enjoyed almost 25 years of fame and some money and died at age 101. Even Governor Nelson Rockefeller claimed her 100th birthday "Grandma Moses" day in the state. After her death the prices of her paintings continued to climb with the highest selling for $1.2M in 1976, 15 years after her passing.

Tim and Nina Zagat

The husband-and-wife team behind the popular dining surveys of the same name were corporate lawyers when they first started printing their restaurant guides. Eventually the guides became so popular that Tim left his job as corporate counsel for Gulf & Western to manage the business in 1986 when he was 51 years old. Nina eventually left the corporate law world to work on the dining surveys as well.

Their web site shares the history: "What began as a hobby grew to become the world's leading consumer survey-based leisure information source. In 1979, Nina and Tim Zagat were at a dinner party with friends and during the meal one of the dinner guests started complaining about the restaurant reviews in a major newspaper. Everyone agreed that the paper's reviews were unreliable so Tim suggested taking a survey of their friends. This led to 200 amateur critics rating and reviewing 100 top restaurants for food, décor, service and cost. The results, printed on legal-sized paper, were an instant success with copies being scooped up all over town."

They were bought by Google in 2011 with terms not disclosed, but experts estimated that Google paid $100 million to $200 million for the publication. Nina Zagat, remained with the business.

To get a model like this from concept to success takes guts, tenacity, and a little bit of luck. The Zagat's efforts to find a publisher for their guide were met with rejection. "And we had very good contacts," Tim Zagat shares. "The law firms where we worked had publishing houses that we were close to, but most national publishers don't like local books, and the track record of publishing restaurant guides up to that time had not been very good." Even a family member in the book business turned them down, and so they decided to print and sell it themselves and sold it from the trunk of their car. They sold 7,500 copies the first year, and 18,000 the second. So imagine that *you* are a high-powered, high falutin' New York attorney. Would you be so driven and so bold as to sell books from your trunk? That's what it takes some times.

Ronald Reagan: actor? And he did some other things

President Ronald Reagan was an actor and wasn't elected to public office until he was 55. I think his legacy and heritage speaks for itself beyond that and he is considered one of the best Presidents in history.

Sadly, the down economy has put a lot of workers over age 50 in the unenviable position of needing to find a new profession. Don't believe that old cliché about middle-aged dogs (not old) *not* learning new tricks, though; lots of wildly successful people found big success in careers they began after their fiftieth birthdays.

There are many more not so famous success stories and they could be in your own backyard. Aside from the age factor many times these success stories have had to overcome many different types of adversity, some financial and some just as deadly.

Some others that didn't necessarily start late, but didn't hit it big until late include:
Henry Ford: While Ford is today known for his innovative assembly line and American-made cars, he wasn't an instant success. In fact, his early businesses failed and left him broke five times before he founded the successful Ford Motor Company.

R. H. Macy: Most people are familiar with this large department store chain, but Macy didn't always have it easy. Macy started seven failed business before finally hitting big with his store in New York City.

Winston Churchill: This Nobel Prize-winning, twice-elected Prime Minster of the United Kingdom wasn't always as well regarded as he is today. Churchill struggled in school and failed the sixth grade. After school he faced many years of political failures, as he was defeated in every election for public office until he finally became the Prime Minister at the ripe old age of 62.

If you're looking for excuses for not pursuing your dream, just count the candles on your birthday cake. Of course, there will always be plenty of reasons for not following through, but ask successful entrepreneurs what's the right age for launching a business, and they'll say: *right now*.

Other expert's words of wisdom:

"Your age can work in your favor, says Jean Biri, author of a blog on early stage entrepreneurship. "It's never too early. Youth allows mental flexibility and a fresh perspective, and it's never too late. Mature self-starters have an edge in minimizing risk and in being taken seriously by investors, lenders, customers and other stakeholders who value experience."

Don Bracken, author of *Career of Gold*, shares, "Still scared? Good. Fear, anxiety and stress are universal to all ages. I don't believe a business can survive without them." Don is past 50 and recently launched his own company, History Publishing, and shares, "Fear of the unknown is natural. If you don't have that, your emotional system is on the blink. Dealing with it is a question of courage, confidence, acceptance of what life throws at you and the willingness to deal with it. Anxiety is necessary to compete. And stress—well, without it, not much is happening."

Scott Burns, former financial writer for the *Dallas Morning News* for over 20 years was offered a buyout that would have allowed him to settle into a leisurely retirement, with ample time to write an occasional book, but the idea for an Internet-based investment business kept buzzing in his head. The more he thought about it, the more he wanted to take the plunge. "The attraction of starting an investment-advisor firm was enormous," he says. So a few months shy of his 66th birthday, he launched AssetBuilder. Within two years, the company secured more than \$125 million in business from 300 clients in 24 states.

A major lesson he learned: one person shouldn't- *can't-* run a business alone. That theme will run the course of this book. Scott is a happy, working Boomer, and his friends say he looks happier and healthier than he ever did in his job.

Entrepreneurs of all ages share the fear of financial failure. Some Gen Ys worry about debt or lost chances in the corporate world; Boomers lose sleep at the prospect of seeing their nest egg disappear. Get used it, these fears, though somewhat real, can be overcome.

I made an effort to interview one of our greatest actors today, Morgan Freeman, for the book, but he was unavailable. In lieu of that, here is his insight to Late Stage success: "The fact that acclaim came late in life doesn't bother me. Success comes when it comes. I had a career for 30 years; a 30-year career is not bad. I often think I'm probably lucky that I wasn't a wild success early on, coming up through the 1970s. I could have very easily burned out." He will be 75 in June, 2012.

(5) How the Phases intersect, collide- and merge: Stephanie Corey

Not all phases are so clearly defined as to say, "I made it in Phase I, II, or III." And sometimes the lines between entrepreneurs that are born to do it themselves or what I call "accidental entrepreneurs" is likewise not so clear,

A great example is **Stephanie Corey** from the San Francisco Bay area of California. She set the stage in Phase One, but really found her calling after she hit 30. Always an overachiever, she came to California from Pennsylvania and already had a solid work ethic and a Bachelors and Masters degree in Economics which she got at age 23. Though not a lawyer by training or degree she worked in the legal area of HP (Hewlett-Packard) in Silicon Valley and earned a six figure income by the time she was 29.

Working in corporate America is a great incubator for many and it sometimes proves that that is NOT the place to be. Corporate policies, bureaucracy, discrimination; they all are prevalent to some degree, more so the larger the company. Speaking for myself personally, this was a track I never was interested in running on. Radicals do NOT make it in a heavy corporate world and internal dissatisfaction and external pressure to "fit in" drive some to the point of anxiety or departure. That is what Stephanie did when she left at 37. She acknowledged, "I reached a position where I could go not further. I didn't have the law degree and I either had to resign myself to staying where I was, being demoted or transferred to another department, or going out on top. I chose to go out on top."

She started in her twenties, and now was ready to venture into entrepreneurship in her thirties. She shared her journey of having conversations with her girlfriends and associates about what to do and what kind of business to start. Maybe a restaurant? A bakery? What ideas have been successful for wives and mothers in their thirties? She had a much stronger business foundation than the majority of entrepreneurs since she saw first hand how a successful Fortune 500 company can and should be run.

Inspiration can come from the most unlikely of places-they are everywhere. A NEW IDEA is born daily and sometimes they are executed upon, but in most cases they flitter away never to be pursued. Stephanie's inspiration came from her son. Her 8 year old son. Her 8 year old son that had an unnatural fear. Of Zombies. Yes, as much as we think (know?) they are fictional, to a young child even irrational fears have realities in their world. Stephanie is unsure why or how her son's fear materialized, but "it may have come from the movie "I am Legend with Will Smith."

How it manifested itself was that Stephanie's son was afraid to go to bed for fear of the Zombie's attack. This fear, like many other irrational fears of children, is very common. Whether they are afraid of Goblins or Ghouls or Creatures of the Night, the majority of parents deal with it and try to rationalize with their kids that "those creatures don't really exist." That approach has varying degrees of success and in most cases the fear eventually goes away. Stephanie tried an unconventional approach, one that engaged me enough to include her story along with many others out there who became customers. She found one of her many cans of fragrances that she had around the house, a lavender scent, and went to her computer to create a label that said "Zombie Repellant." "Zombies are icky and don't like sweet smells", she explained to her son, "and if you spray your room they will be afraid to enter." A likely story Mom, but regardless her son sprayed the crap out of that room! In all the corners — and especially on the door handle — and of course under the bed. That spray made the difference between being afraid to go to bed and getting a good night's sleep. She decided to experiment with different scents that were available and to engage a professional graphics designer to create a label. "Fortunately I had a neighbor that was a brilliant and creative designer and what we use today is pretty much what we came up with at the beginning."

She made up some labels, stuck them on same spray bottles and shared them with friends to get their opinion. After they stopped laughing they tried it with their young kids and had great results. This irrational fear of going to bed at night is quite common and can be a real ordeal, but it is an every-night affair in millions of homes.

She thought to herself, "I may have a business here," and decided to pursue it. She talked with many that she trusted including the straight and narrow minded (or so we think) of those in her former legal department at work. When they *too* stopped laughing they mostly told her she had a great and unique idea and encouraged her to continue. This is where most will stop. They will stop due to lack of focus, vision, insight, money, confidence; the list is endless. Now that she had a label, Stephanie decided to seek out a manufacture of custom fragrances and found one in Michigan. She called, and when *they also* stopped laughing, they said that they could create — and bottle — whatever she wanted in a scent. With a minimum order of just 100 bottles and an annual commitment of 500 the first year, Stephanie took on the challenge. And created several unique smells guaranteed to keep monsters at bay.

In less than one year she has expanded her product line to include not just fragrances, but also created "characters" and named her business "Miss Stephanie's Potions." The business is *not* named after her, but instead created a fictional owner of the business also named Stephanie. It's just a coincidence. Really?

From her web site: "Miss Stephanie is a Voodoo Medicine Woman who studied in a small town in Louisiana. Long ago, Miss Stephanie specialized in preparing potions to cure common ailments. During one particularly bad Louisiana storm, Miss Stephanie was up late preparing a healing tea for one of the locals when a knock came at the door. There in the doorway stood a large, very ugly and very smelly zombie! Miss Stephanie slammed the door in his face and quickly whipped up one of her potions. When that persistent zombie knocked again, Miss Stephanie was prepared, spray in hand. Sure enough, the zombie went running to tell all his friends that the town's medicine woman created a potion strong enough to turn all those pesky ghouls into sweet, friendly creatures. The next day, the wise medicine woman created potions for all the local townspeople, and that night, all the children slept peacefully. Today, Miss Stephanie continues creating products that empower children to take charge of their fears and deal with their anxieties naturally." Ha, a likely story!

From there came monsters such as Draco, Fleabane, Mugwort and others. And you can be sure more will be created. Her line of sprays include "Monster be Good, along with Vampire, Zombie and Werewolf be Good" (you never know what a kid may be afraid of!) and even a spray designed to attract good fairies called "Essence of Fairy Dust."

All this came from the imagination and ingenious mind of someone that did not have a business idea to start, but got an inspiration and saw it through. What inspirations have you had in your life that you never acted upon? What can you be inspired to create if you actually seek out a niche market?

Stephanie also has stayed true to her convictions as a business owner and conscientious American. "All our products are made in the United States and everything is 100% natural. If I wouldn't expose my son to it I wouldn't want to expose anyone's children to it," she shared.

What does the future hold for Miss Stephanie and her World of Potions? Along with the many fragrances she now also has:

- Bath and Body lotions and repellant for the baths that kids never want to take
- A line of t-shirts and pajamas with the characters on the front

And the one I think really sets her apart is a line of stuffed toys in the likeness of the characters she created, all seven of them. Kids can now keep the Zombies away by taking a bath with repellant, spraying the room, sleeping in Zombie-proof PJs, and holding on to their favorite characters while they sleep. She has truly expanded and repurposed with an "off the wall idea that everyone laughed at" and has done this in less than one year. She has surrounded herself with a TEAM of experts and is running this like a business- from her home. Her line is sold in several stores in the San Francisco Bay area and her goal "is to be in 100 locations next year" which will be her first full year in business. After invested about $60,000 into the business to date she is having difficulty projecting income since there is really no exact model to follow.

In addition to the sales volume and the number of selling locations, her other major focus is exposure. She has brochures and has spent little on marketing but did get profiled on a well received web site article called "Zombie Apocalypse: Ten Tech Products You Shouldn't Be Without" at www.techlicious.com/guide/zombie-apocalypse-ten-tech-products-you-shouldnt-be-without.

The article focused- tongue in cheek- on the Top Ten things you need in the event of a Zombie Attack. That list also involves products from other "outside the box thinkers" like Zombie GPS (for tracking Zombies) and a 12 volt heater/ cooler for carrying your food since you are always on the go trying to avoid those critters. And here's the kicker. This article was developed after the CDC- the Center for Disease Control- yes the REAL ONE, actually came up with preparedness guide to help in the event of a Zombie infestation. That report can be found at www.cdc.gov/phpr/zombies.htm.

Stephanie ignored those that laughed at her and ignored those that thought she was foolish. Her Mom though it was a great idea, but her Dad, a conservative former surgeon, has no room for unconventional thinkers. To make it at any stage requires a thick skin. The saying is: "Every one loves a winner, but when you lose you lose alone." People will encourage you once you HAVE a winning idea but it may take years- even decades- to find that idea. Many fail, file bankruptcy and lose families in their efforts to succeed. What price are you willing to pay? Financial success is a matter of opinion and personal judgment. Miss Stephanie has reached a point of success that most will not reach and her future appears to be very profitable regardless of how much money she makes. Plus she gets to keep her son safe.

Her contact information: (www.missstephaniespotions.com, Stephanie@MissStephaniesPotions.com)

you'll never leave where you are until you decide where you'd rather be.

(6) A Blue Collar Gen Y winner: Matt Shoup.

Many times when we think about "making it big" we mistakenly believe that we need to come up with some new invention or web site or radical departure from the norm. Can you make it big *quickly* in a business as ordinary as paint contracting? Can low tech businesses that anyone CAN do be your ticket to success?

Matt Shoup out of Loveland, Colorado started a painting company in 2005 at age 25 after being laid off from a corporate position. As much as we sometimes (mistakenly) believe that being an employee offers some degree of stability, that has become less likely over the years. Being fired from a job has led many to become business owners. Some embrace it; some shun it. And some grudgingly give in and try to run a business with varying degrees of success.

Matt was taught early by his parents that if he wanted something he had to do it on my own. "When I was 10 I asked my parents for $200 and they said 'go find a way to make your own money!' which is exactly what I did," he shared. He started a lawn mowing service and later peddled candy out of his middle school locker. "Had my parents given me the $200 I asked for I probably would have never found the ways to make money." He added "I see many that did get the handout and do not know the value of hard work, and the value of earning your dollars." In hindsight he is glad that they made him earn his due.

He founded M & E Painting with just $100 to his name. What drove him was different than many Phase I success stories and that is he HAD to make money. After losing a job that paid six figures he now realized that he had that much or more in outstanding debts. It wasn't just the entrepreneurial spirit- though he certainly had that- but he needed to make a living. Even with a college degree that is no guarantee of success in a corporate world or in an entrepreneurial one, either. After interviewing almost two dozen Gen Y success stories I found that most of them did go to college and completed their degree. Like many college graduates their degrees were in something totally different than how they actually made a living. The overriding pattern I saw from the college experience is that once the Millennials got over the "party all night" mindset of college they applied themselves and saw results. Maybe it was good grades, maybe a degree, but college was a good incubator to focus on a goal. In Matt's case he studied overseas and that experience helped him as it does almost everyone that is so blessed and motivated to do. Matt graduated with a degree in Spanish and one in Human Development and Family Studies. Maybe they help him in his painting business, but probably not.

Another common trait in early success stories is the desire to be "cool", be innovative and show the world you can do it and make a difference. That wasn't the case with Matt.

"For me, being cool was not important. I was more concerned with being able to take care of my family, and challenging myself to say 'Matt, you can do this, go kick some butt and make this happen.' I did have some ego as I was able to become successful and that was put into check." Showing his wisdom and maturity he added "Hitting 30 has really made me look back and see the success, the drivers, and to the question of being cool."

One of the questions I asked all the contributors to this book was "Assuming you were "set" at an early age, what would be your motivation to keep going? Money? Accomplishment? Helping others?"

The not so surprising answers across the board was that most would do exactly what they do because they love it. The "Success Meter" is just a barometer and is subjective at best. Matt's take on that: "My motivation is to inspire others through service. Lead by example and show people that you can be successful by doing this and sticking to your values, and that it is not all about the money. Money is nice, and being able to serve and share it with others is awesome too!"

He is setting a good example since his growth since starting in 2005 has been over 500% and that is impressive considering where the overall economy has been. M & E is now one of the largest paint contracting companies in Northern Colorado with volume in excess of $10M in jobs in less than half a dozen years.

I picked Matt for inclusion in this book because he took a simple business and created an Award Winning Company, which is a concept he teaches. With that as a track record he started a consulting company, "Shoup Consulting" in 2009 with the intention of teaching others how he did it.

Success IS the best teacher and he recently wrote his story called "Become an Award Winning Company" which is sold nationwide, plus he started an organization that teaches other how to do likewise, called "Be an Award Winning Company." He wants to create more Rock Stars. Does he typify the "normal" Gen Y success story? In most ways not at all, but in other ways he sets a great example.

If you do something really, really well, consider teaching others how to do likewise. Writing a book is a logical move and that is what Matt has done. Each business model feeds off the other, and even though they are all different they all carry the same theme: *Entrepreneurialism is good for individuals and for the country as well.*

One of the things that Matt discovered early on and one of the principles he teaches is that most advertising is a waste of money and any business can grow faster by understanding the difference between advertising and PR. Matt has become a master at this and has been profiled in dozens of publications and has received many awards. I won't steal his thunder, but his book is spot on when it comes to getting free advertising by understanding how to work the media.

If you found a business based on solid character and work ethics you can make it. We see this all the time with foreign born business owners that are not spoiled by the "American Way" nor are they lazy. Since Matt found out early from his parents that if he wanted to make it he had to do it on his own, that is exactly what he did.

Matt's contact: (www.mandepainting.com., matt@mandepainting.com)

> # Be yourself.
> There is something
> that you can do
> better than any other.
> Listen to the inward voice
> and bravely obey that.
>
> (Unknown)

(7) A Success story: between Phases II & III

Marlene Caroselli is a Doctor in Education but came late to the entrepreneurial party. She spent many years as a teacher and employee but came from an innovative family with a father that immigrated to the US at age 15 by himself and a mother that, with just an eight grade education, invented a drapery rod in her seventies which was manufactured by Kirsch Drapery Company, a 100 year old manufacturer of drapery products from Lexington, Kentucky. As Louis Pasteur was once quoted, "Chance favors the prepared mind," and Marlene's incentive to jump in to the **Center for Professional Development** came across by "accident", but there really never are any of those. They are usually opportunities that present themselves and are dependent upon how you react to them.

At the age of 41 she was working as a property manager in Los Angeles and one of her tenants was National

University, which offered degree programs for working adults at night and on weekends. She was also teaching there in addition to being the building manager. The Department of Defense called the university one day and asked for a recommendation--they needed someone to teach business writing. The university recommended her and thus began a series of contracts that lasted until her very last, pre-retirement assignment--teaching writing to Navy SEALS just a few years ago. At the same time, many of her students were telling their bosses in Fortune 100 firms about her classes and she began to receive requests from Lockheed-Martin, Northrop-Grumman, and similar aerospace companies. She saw an opportunity and in her words "soon realized entrepreneurship was my destiny."

How would most react to that opportunity? Would they (or you) stay on as an employee with job security and less responsibility?

The Center for Professional Development came out of that fortuitous opportunity and started to offer training products and services to corporations and government agencies, growing to a company with several employees. They developed a long list of courses--over 30—and initially most of them centered around the common theme of communications. Based on requests they expanded into courses related to teamwork, quality control and similar concepts.

As the owner of a teaching school she began to research other methods of teaching and continued her own education, including getting her Doctorate in Education. She began to write, first one book then many more, but did not publish her first until almost age **50**. Since then she has been most prolific and now has 60 books to her credit, including "Hiring and Firing" and "Principled

Persuasion" which was named a Director's Choice by Doubleday Book Club. She sold her company to devote all her time to writing and speaking and is a keynote speaker and trainer throughout the country.

As I got to know her she shared some insights to how entrepreneurship can become a powerful magnet at any age, especially as we approach Phase III. "The fear of being bored is a terrific incentive to remain occupied, to continue learning, to avoid stagnation" she said and added "I think the drive to success is more focused and more realistic in later years."

Finding late stage Boomer success stories was more challenging than finding those that succeeded early in life. With such a youth-centric society that we have, there are great accolades and press poured on the Young Successful Business owners. The ones that are harder to find are the ones that do not make it in their twenties, their thirties or even their forties. What drives someone to keep trying to grab that brass ring in to their fifth decade??

To reach Marlene: (www.saatchionline.com/LainaCelano, mccpd@frontiernet.net)

(8) A Healthy Millennial: Tiffany Prinster

Success sometimes comes early, but not always easily. Tiffany Prinster is a partner in DIY HCG Inc, a company which teaches diet techniques and sells a product called "HCG". Human chorionic gonadotrophin (**hCG**) is a glycoprotein hormone produced during pregnancy that is made by the developing embryo after conception. It is a product that borders the very thin line between a *pharmaceutical* (regulated) product and a *homeopathic* (natural) one. It can be a gray area when it comes to regulations and currently the FDA is clamping down on HCG sellers. The United States Food and Drug Administration has stated that this drug is fraudulent and ineffective for weight loss. It is also not protected as a homeopathic drug and has been deemed an illegal substance. That is causing Tiffany's once million dollar business to be in jeopardy. Which we'll get to in a moment.

Let's find out how this all came about and what lessons can be learned.

From their web site: "DIY HCG, Inc. was started by Linda Prinster and Tiffany Prinster in December of 2008 to help people with the HCG diet. Linda started 'Pounds and Inches Away' in 2007, which is an HCG diet consulting firm, and had thousands of successful clients. In September of 2008, Tiffany joined Pounds and Inches Away to work as a consultant. Tiffany was actively involved in the HCG diet forums and noticed the need for homeopathic HCG drops online. So, Linda and Tiffany decided to launch DIYHCG.com since they already had a significant amount of experience in successfully helping others to complete the HCG diet successfully."

It started off as a small, call-to-order site. Then, in February of 2009, DIY HCG moved up to a big, new e-commerce site. At that point, Tiffany was doing most everything involved in the business: taking phone calls; fulfilling online orders; packing all the boxes; driving them to the post office each day; updating the website; answering customer e-mails; answering support calls, and everything else. Many of you can relate.

The Diet and Weight Loss industries are BIG business in the United States and getting bigger all the time. There are many competitors and they all tout their techniques as being the best, etc... So how do you separate yourselves from them, show you are credible and most important, provide results? HCG has proven to be an effective technique for losing weight but it is not a stand alone solution and must be incorporated into a fairly strict diet of less than 1000 calories per day. That in itself should allow weight loss, but if it can be improved by adding HCG into the mix, even better.

Tiffany and her Mom started small, started locally and then private labeled (put their own brand on the label, also called "white labeling") their HCG drops and went on-line. Their business grew and grew and if you visit their web site you will see that Tiffany is the face and voice of the company and has created wonderful videos (www.diyHCG.com).

The reality is, sometimes your business must change and in some cases you may be forced to change. In this case the catalyst was regulation and that could happen to many industries. If you sell a product or service that later is deemed "illegal" or "not recommended", suddenly you are out of business. My primary reason for including their profile is because they created something, and it became successful. They hired and grew and thought it was smooth sailing. They thought they were set. In May, 2011 they encountered their first major setback when Google and Yahoo refused to run their on-line advertising due to the FDA's position. The major search engines are very sensitive to offering anything deemed (or perceived to be) illegal, so their Number One portal for sales was no longer available. Imagine that you had the back cover of the New York Times every Sunday and suddenly they said you could no longer have it? That is effectively what happens when your on-line presence is shut down. Granted the FDA's position affected all sellers of HCG the same, but that made no difference to Tiffany's business.

The second shoe fell in December, 2011 when the FDA contacted the manufacturers of the HCG products and per Tiffany, "scared the manufacturers enough so that now they no longer produce the homeopathic HCG." Few businesses will intentionally take on the government or regulatory agencies, so for now HCG manufactures are unwilling to make their products any longer. They are willing to make an alternative that is without the hormone they took issue with, but that solution is much less effective. The irony is, the hormone is "present in pregnant women everyday for 9 months at much, much higher quantities," per Tiffany. There are some lesser known manufacturers that continue to make the HCG that Tiffany sold, but there is some question as to their purity and effectiveness and Tiffany is unwilling to put their customers at risk.

The future is uncertain and there is growing backlash from the public and those that have been pleased with the results of their HCG diet plan. Many have been stockpiling their own cache at home and there are on-line petitions and movements looking to overturn the FDA's decision. On Tiffany's web site they provide links for the protest and hope to be part of a grass root's movement to turn things around. The FDA's position has had a ripple effect, from the manufacturers to the wholesalers to the retail distributors. Tiffany has been forced to lay off employees and looking to create lemonade out of lemons.

Though Tiffany is half way through the first phase of her business life when I posed the question of "what lessons she had learned already" she was most prolific and gave me her Top Ten list of lessons she learned after just a few years. I find them insightful and these tenets can be applied to any business.

1. You have to believe in your product and have a good product or service that people actually *need or want* (author's emphasis). If you are just in it to make money, you will get nowhere.
2. Make sure your have your financial reporting in place early. We started without good financials which is fine when you are having great months,

but in the slower months, you MUST know what money you have available.

3. DON'T HIRE FAMILY. You (like me) probably think that your family is different and that you love each other enough to make it through working together. I can tell you firsthand after having family members as partners and employees that it is NOT worth the pain and strain on your familial relationships. It's NOT worth it.

4. Make sure you make your mark in the marketing area of your company. My one regret in the business is that I didn't spend the money to establish ourselves as the biggest and the best HCG company early enough. Soon I was run over by competitors with worse service and higher prices only because they threw a TON of money into online advertising.

5. If someone isn't working out as an employee, get rid of them as soon as you know that to be the case. Negative attitudes and behaviors spread like a cancer.

6. Get ready to be the bad guy sometimes. You can't always go around like a nice, magical fairy who is never mean and always delivering positive news. You will need to discipline and have uncomfortable conversations. You will need to fire people. And you will need to make unpopular decisions. Just get used to it or get out the position.

7. Surround yourself with FANTASTIC people. This kind of goes back to # 5, but make sure everyone around you is working at the same level. If someone falls behind, talk with them about it and give them a chance to adjust. If they don't, you need to let them go (of course work with someone who knows about HR before you do let them go since that decision could come back to bite you).

8. Always work with CLEAR, definitive contracts and have your attorney look them over before signing.
9. Check references and Google a business before working with a new company. That could save you hundreds of thousands in the end.
10. Finally, TRUST YOUR GUT. If someone or something doesn't feel right, follow that instinct. Again, it could save you tons of money, heartache, and energy in the end

Those are wonderful pieces of advice from anyone at any age!

In closing her story I wanted to share one of the other survey questions I asked which was "when you see others your age do you believe that they should have the same motivations to 'succeed' as you?" That same question can be asked of any person in any stage, but I thought her response transcended all of them: "NO. I know that I am different. I always have been. I don't expect that any of my friends my age be like that. The only time I think a little differently is when people my age complain that they can't afford things or can't do this or that when I KNOW that they could if they would just believe in themselves, use their talents, and put their minds to it. *There are always excuses to not do something."*

So what is your excuse? Here is a 25 year-old women that created a business, took it to high profile and success in less than two years, and now finds herself having to reinvent her business model already. I have no doubt that she will find a new path and recover and in short order be better and bigger than ever.

FAIL
[F] FIRST
[A] ATTEMPT
[I] IN
[L] LEARNING

(9) Anthony Saladino: A Gen Y that got it right

Selling kitchen cabinets seems to be a sure fire road to success and riches, right? No, not really. What I found in many of the Gen Y success stories is that they took a commonplace, even mundane business and created a profitable venture. And I specifically wanted to focus on ones that anyone at any *age* could take on. They don't need a lot of money, nor technical skills; just a determination to know the product, the customer and how to cater to them and offer the best service possible.

Anthony Saladino, age 29, started Kitchen Cabinet Kings two years ago when he was 27, and lived in New York City. Like many others he got fired from his position as a designer of kitchen cabinets and realized that there is no security in working for someone else. "After being abruptly fired, I decided that I would never put my fate in someone else's hands again. I decided the best way to control my own destiny would be to create my own business." Haven't we all had that feeling if were ever unfortunate enough to be laid off? Some might consider a business like this would take a lot of money and material and employees, but Anthony has made it simple, generating sales and income within his first month, which is very impressive.

A little background on kitchen cabinets.

I can speak from personal experience since I had my kitchen cabinets redone several years ago. The process went like this:

A designer came to my come, took measurements, showed us pictures of various colors and styles and gave me a quote. It wasn't cheap. For me personally I had the company do the install, but that was my choice. I could have done it myself or hired a contractor to do it, both of which would have been cheaper. Anthony's company, Kitchen Cabinet Kings caters to those that want to take the later position. Most of his cabinetry is off the shelf and fairly standardized. You pull out and discard the old cabinets and install the new. As long as you have accurate measurements it's really like putting a round peg in a round hole.

What impressed me about Anthony's model is that he has very few employees, uses independent contractors and does business nationwide. That is a model that I was not aware existed and I told him for me personally, living in California I would not order cabinets from New York. But here's the secret. The cabinets don't come out of New York. They come from a host of different factories all over the country. He shared that "California is his fourth biggest market and he has sold cabinets as far away as Alaska." When I countered that shipping costs would be a deterrent to me ordering cabinets from afar he said that shipping costs are minimized and the weight is not so great that it becomes a deal killer. Most cabinetry today is plywood or pressed wood with a laminate finish so it is much lighter than traditional oak or solid wood cabinets. And that is OK. He caters to the low-to-mid market, not the custom homes or high-end materials. "My plan is to have factories all over the United States that I contract shipping 'off the shelf' cabinetry to the local markets. That reduces shipping costs and shipping time," he stated.

Kitchen Cabinet Kings is run out of a small office in Manhattan, but that is more of a headquarters than an actual working office. With executive suites and virtual offices you can maintain an address wherever you please and actually work out of a more affordable location. Anthony's brother, Andrew, who is even younger (age 24), is an integral part of the Cabinet Kings model. Andrew is the Chief Operating Officer and runs the on-line and social media presence of the company. When someone thinks of e-commerce they usually think of a web based company selling products via some type of shopping cart. Anthony and his brother have an e-commerce company that sells cabinets. Not quite as sexy, but very profitable.

They have taken a commanding lead in the New York City metropolitan area, but do most of their business outside the Northeast. Effectively acting as a broker for kitchen and bath cabinets, they can locate their offices anywhere and do business anywhere. This was not Anthony's first business, since his first one, called Colors of NY, failed. "That company offered various art services to my local NYC market. This company failed due to my inexperience in this field and poor partner selection," he confided. The entrepreneurial lessons come quickly at any age and when I asked him what lessons he had learned he came back with "I've learned that no one in this world will hand you success. If you want to succeed, you are going to have to step up and take it." So true.

One of the focuses of this book while in development was understanding the differentiators between Phase I success and the others and the importance of the "coolness" factor at that stage. In later phases you become successful because you've learned hard lessons and had failures or because you must make a living. There are some Millennials that do things for those reasons but many do it because it makes them more significant and stand out amongst their peers. Not so with Anthony. "My decision to accomplish my goals had nothing to do with being cool. I was "cool" in my younger years and had countless friends. My drive to succeed was purely financial. When I was fired, I had high monthly living expenses, low savings and no one willing to help me financially. It was either sink or swim and I choose the later. However, the attention I've received from my awards and media publications is kind of cool, but was not a factor when starting my business."

Anthony attended college, both the College of Staten Island and State University of Albany, and earned his degree in Sociology, but that was not a factor in his career choice. It taught him focus and showed him options, but his entrepreneurial drive was stronger than any degree could offer. In his second full year of operation they did $1.1 million in gross sales and he believes in year three he could do 50-100% better than that. Must you be a high-tech wizard or guru to tap into the potential of on-line marketing? Decide for yourself.

Anthony's contact:: (www.kitchencabinetkings.com)

"Unless you try to do something beyond what you have already mastered, you will never grow."
Ronald E. Osborn

(10) Katie Hughes: A PhD Gen Y that never needed her degree

What does having a PhD in Solid State Chemistry have to do with starting a company that offers a unique solution for exercisers with bad knees? Not a darn thing. Yet Katie Hughes from Charlotte, NC is an example of where a need showed her how to offer a solution. Her many years of education, which we'll get to in a moment, were helpful in cognitive thinking and designing a product that would fix a problem, but it was her entrepreneurial drive that made the difference.

In addition to being a brilliant 30-year old Katie is also a fitness instructor and teaches a technique known as "Zumba," a Latin inspired dance fitness program that was developed in the 90's. It has proven to be very popular and trendy since it incorporates many fun dance regimens including salsa, hip-hop, mambo and even some Bollywood, martial arts and belly dancing moves. It appeals primarily to women and has provided a social engagement for students as well as an exercise routine.

Any physical fitness regimen can cause injuries or challenges but the complaints from Zumba students and instructors were very specific: knee problems. Most students use a traditional aerobic or gym shoe which has tread on the bottom for traction, which is what they were designed to do. Zumba moves include a lot of twists and turns and hip-hop movements, and in many cases the "stickiness" of the shoes is an issue which causes excessive torque and creates knee injuries. The knee joint can be very unforgiving and even healthy students- athletic or not- can take that one move too far and create a small tear or tenderness in the knee joint. There are special shoes made especially for "sliding " motions, one that creates less drag or friction, but many new students are resistant to getting a special shoe just for a specific exercise. It is similar to those that become committed to bicycle riding with their unique "clip on" pedals. They also require a special shoe, but most people who commit to that degree have an insight as to whether they intend to become serious riders. Since Zumba is new to most students, they are reluctant and rarely will commit to spending the money on Zumba shoes since they can run from $75 to well over $100. She did her homework and went to the Zumba instructor's message boards and blogs and saw that this was a common complaint with them, too.

Katie heard these many complaints and looked into alternative solutions. "Since the Zumba movement is a twist on the hips and knees, is there anything available to wear over the shoe to reduce the friction and create a more frictionless surface?" was the question she asked herself. Her scientific background allowed her to look at this like an experiment; a hypothesis, just as a scientist would objectively look at a problem seeking an answer. She found none, so used her drive to start a business to develop one. After spending years in the academic world and reaching the pinnacle of graduate degrees she specifically wanted to start a business, but had no idea what to do. It need not be related to her scientific background or credentials, so she was wide open to possibilities. Her father was a business owner and built high-end race car engines, but the flaw in his plan was that his success was based on his personal efforts. "Watching my father run the business, I realized that I would need to delegate much more than he did if I was to achieve the lifestyle that I hoped for. Because money was tight, he tended to do a lot of the work for the business himself even if he didn't really enjoy some of the jobs. Because I started the business while working full time, I had little choice but to delegate when my plate was full. Delegation is a skill of necessity." A great way to start creating a business- with the focus of scalability and growth- plus it also validates the mindsets of the Gen Ys who *do not* want their businesses to be their lives, unlike many Boomers that let their businesses define them.

Katie conceived and came up with a sleeve or wrap that can be placed around the shoe. She tried different materials, elasticities and took into account the "sticking factor" since that was the goal. She came up with some samples, tried them out and shared with her fellow Zumba instructors. Initial results and feedback was good so she sought out a manufacturer- really just a seamstress- that had heavy duty equipment to sew the "slip-on dancers" together. She also saw an avenue for marketing since the slip-ons could possibly be labeled with a sponsor, right? Could it be sold to Zumba or larger gyms? These were questions that required an answer.

She came up with a design that worked and then to came the critical decision: Does she spend $5,000 to buy a booth at a Zumba Convention, and spend the time and money to go and sell her product? If so, how many does she make and take? How much do you invest on an untested product?

I'll pause for a second since I have been and seen many come to this critical juncture. To invest $5,000 and more to market a mostly untested idea to an unknowing market is a huge risk. And most will fail. Conventions and trade shows are crowded with many distractions and you have but seconds to get the attention of those passing by. But she did! She had lines and buzz and sold out of her supply of over 1500 pairs of Slip-on Dancers that she brought along, plus made some great connections. The instructors that were *there* at the convention used the product at the demo classes and they caught peoples' attention. So *this* story does have a happy ending for now. Her goal was exposure and support and possibly to engage the other instructors to become her sales force. She was successful and I told her quite candidly that she is one of the few to actually pull this off, get her money back and even make a little money on the first go round.

Her credibility as a Zumba instructor was invaluable since she carried experience and that helped her relate to many of her fellow instructors. She launched this idea in October, 2009 and in 2010, her first full year she did about $60,000 in sales and in 2011 it quadrupled to about $350,000. She initially went to Zumba, got a provisional patent and offered to partner with them. Her response from Zumba: "thanks, but no thanks" and they were the ones that suggested getting a booth at the convention. In hindsight it may have been much better that she was *not* embraced by Zumba since she now has the potential to make much more money, but more important, she keeps control. Never see failure as failure, but as a chance to learn.

She now has a local (U.S.) manufacturer and has sold over 15,000 bands. They retail for just under $15, so that is impressive by any extent. She is now looking to repurpose her product and find other revenue and distribution possibilities. One of the other smart things she did was take classes on business and people management. She acknowledges that as a scientist they tend to work in solitary confines so learning how to manage a staff in expectation of future growth is wise. In the past year she has left her job and is devoting 100% of her time on her company. Again, *her* company. Projections and plans for the new year include a children's market and venturing into additional dance/ exercise programs like Jazzercise and even ballet. Dance has become very popular over the past decade and many Top 10 reality shows are dance specific. Many people create their own home videos and show off their dance moves. Is there a market there for them? She's not sure yet since targeting home users is more difficult but much larger. And even high tech companies like Wii, made by Nintendo, offer a Wii Zumba "game" for home use, so they must know something and see potential.

Can anyone at any age come up with such an innovative product? Katie had advanced degrees and a doctorate, but that made no difference in the genesis and future of the Slip-on Dancers. If you are over 40, or over 50, or older than that, there is no reason that you cannot find a pain, a need, and find or create a solution.

Katie's contact: www.slipondancers.com, khughes@slipondancers.com

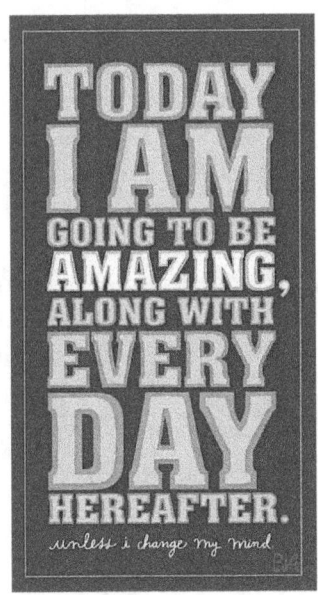

When I asked Tim if anyone could do what he did he responded "Absolutely." I shared with him that I chose him to profile because what he did involved no high-tech talent, but was something "ordinary" which anyone *could* do. I immediately apologized for referring to his skills as ordinary and thought my remark was rude. His response: "No, please call me ordinary! What I did anyone could do and I am no one special and was unbelievably lucky." Does that sound like a businessman that has his ego in check? I believe so, but it wasn't always so and Timothy had his own demons to vanquish. Success at an early age sometimes takes its toll and even though he made millions before he was legally able to drink he didn't blow it on expensive cars and toys like many others he has seen. He did take his fraternity buddies out for a party when he had a successful "score", but because none of them could drink either it was less than a grand.

When and how did Tim go off track? Before we get to that let's review where he started.

If Timothy's story wasn't real it could almost be a fictional screenplay since it began when he was thirteen years old. At that age he had his Bar Mitzvah, the Jewish ceremony that is transitional for boys to emerge as men. Customarily there is a celebration with family, friends and in lieu of gifts many give the Bar Mitzvah boy money. Tim got $12,415 in gift money and told his parents he wanted to invest it in the stock market since it was going crazy in the late 90's as we may recall. His parents were glad of his interests but concerned since they questioned whether their child had enough experience in such ventures, but concluded it was better than blowing it on something frivolous. Their position was that if he lost it, it would be a hard yet valuable lesson learned. He was a quick study and by the time he graduated from high school he made lots of money- millions of dollars- by investing in one of the sectors that many "professional" investors shun and belittle: Penny Stocks.

Penny Stocks are ones that have little value and are priced at less than $1.00 per share. They are tempting to buy since you can get so many shares for so little money and for just $100 you can buy 200 shares of a stock selling for just $.50. That same $200 will buy you just one third of one share of Google and in many cases $100 will not get you in the traditional investing market at all. Investors like these are usually novices and cater to the volume theory of owning many shares and not just value shares. These Penny Stocks are "thinly traded" which means there is not a big market in them and their values unfortunately can easily be manipulated. Some companies that may offer shares like this have been known to publicize some kind of significant breakthrough or event- sometimes fraudulently- and a $.50 stock *can* go to $2.00 within minutes. The dollars may be small but that is a 400% increase and when that happens the "pump and dump" crowd comes in, takes their money and laughs all the way to the bank.

These transactions are more regulated than in years past but can still be risky. In Timothy's case they were his road to riches. From his $12,415 investment at 13 he accumulated $1.85 million before he graduated from college and at age 22 was well ahead of many if not most investors.

As the saying goes, ignorance can be bliss, but Timothy was not ignorant of finances, just of the "ways of the world" and certain aspects of life. "When you're young you don't know how difficult the world can be, so your naiveté incentivizes you differently because you do it for the glory and are able to dream big. Adults realize how complex the world is so even small achievements that can pay bills are worth striving for."

Like many other successful business owners the money was not really the prize, but merely a marker on the road to wealth. For Tim, "It was a video game for a long time and the money I made was simply a way of keeping track of my score...I wanted the high score and despite my making a few million dollars not just once but twice within a few years, I was confident and had expensive tastes."

His journey went off track- way off track- around 2005 when he started to get publicity and let success go to his head. His strategy had always been that he would only trade when his chosen stocks hit *new highs*, but when the economy began to falter in the mid 2000's he started ignoring his own rules and lost about one-third of his portfolio. His venture into short selling was a costly mistake that caused him to start drinking. His previously down to earth mindset went awry and he spent much of his time in a state of clinical depression and drunken stupor. He is very candid about sharing the troubles that he endured, but used it as a learning lesson and a crossroad to get him straight. In 2006 a Reality TV financial program aired called "Wall Street Warriors" which profiled whiz kids (including Tim) that were making it big in finance. Finally after all those years of trying to get noticed he did, yet was in a depressed state of mind to deal with it. The show ran for 2.5 years and has been off the air since 2008, but Timothy got great publicity and notoriety out of it. Unfortunately during the many times he was on the show he was drunk. In his words, "Most financial shows have boring guests and I was so high that I didn't care. I was a huge hit. People loved how funny and flip I was about it and I became a break-out star. It made me as infamous as I was famous."

He dealt with it until he realized that his failure was his own doing and by ignoring the rules that had made him successful all those prior years he knew that *he* was the underlying cause. "When I realized that I was *not a loser*, but my new *approach* was, I jumped out of it, went back to what worked and started making money again," he shared. Even prior to this downturn he realized that he was prone to going off track so when he went to college- even though he didn't require the degree or the education- he majored in Philosophy just to get some grounding. "To thine own self be true" as Shakespeare once said, so knowing your weakness- in addition to your strengths- is a huge game changer. Ironically Tim acknowledges he is not a good student and has flunked the securities exam- twice. Not necessarily book smart, but certainly street smart and investment savvy.

Since he hit his highs and worked though his lows he wanted to share his experience with others, primarily since the Internet gurus and financial wizards were mostly selling crap. As Wall Street and the rest of the economy faltered he got disgusted that many were taking advantage of the Greater Fool theory so he began publishing his own newsletters, guides and videos and later wrote *"An American Hedge Fund: How I Made $2 Million as a Stock Operator & Created a Hedge Fund"* which exposed the con men that were profiting from the short selling of penny stocks.

At this point he only trades on his own personal account and not for others, but instead teaches others how to do what he does. His publishing business, "Millionaire

Media, LLC" is much more profitable than his trading and allows him to create a sustainable future income. About 10% of his income comes from his own efforts and 90% comes from his growing media publishing business. He also employs both his parents along with 23 more, a five-fold increase from his year prior. Considering he just passed 30, has an apartment in Connecticut and New York, Timothy is in a great place in his life and encourages others- regardless of age- to be innovative and think with unconventional ideas.

What keeps him going even though he doesn't need the money? What advice can he offer? "Everyone has different values, so if you want to make it and you don't succeed that's very disappointing, but it's the majority of the people in the world. I know that 75% of people hate their jobs so I wish they could all make it; nothing's worse than being old and filled with regret. However some people just want to live a healthy and balanced life so they don't need to make it. I envy them, but my drive pushes me forward at all times, and whether I make it or not, I cannot stop." Are entrepreneurs born or are they made? Can some people *not* follow their dreams? You can answer that question on your own.

Timothy's information: www.timothysykes.com

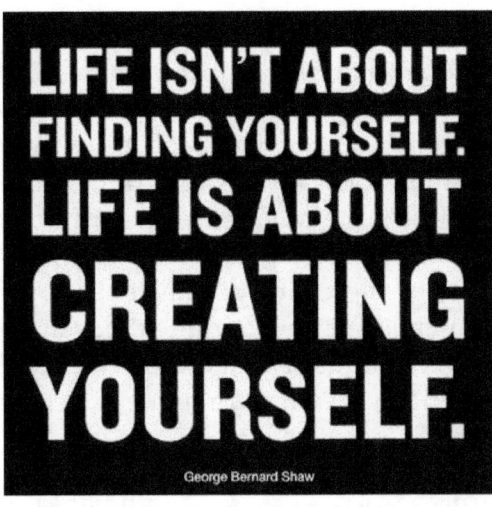

LIFE ISN'T ABOUT FINDING YOURSELF. LIFE IS ABOUT CREATING YOURSELF.

George Bernard Shaw

(12) Success at any age: Tori Scott, fulfilling her dreams in Phase III.

As they say on television, "I'm not really a doctor I just play one on TV," Tori Scott is not really Tori Scott: she is really Pam Payne, a 57 year-old writer from Dallas, Texas. Tori Scott is her nom be plume, or pen name that many writers use to mask their true identity. Sometimes it is done because the writer wants to remain discreet if they are revealing hidden information; sometimes it is used when a writer of a certain genre wants to segue way into something else without revealing their history. Stephen King is a great example as he has written several books under a different name (two actually) and written on different genres. And sometimes it is done because the author wants to become someone else; someone that the reader of the book will be more interested in reading. That is the case with Tori Scott, also known as Pam Payne.

By Googling Tori Scott I found over 27,000 hits and she is a prolific writer of "romance novels" with five completed and on the market right now. At age 57 years old she may not fit the stereotypical image of a writer of young women's material, but she is proud of her history- plus she's a romantic- and shares on her web bio: "Best Selling and award-winning author Tori Scott believes in love. She met her husband, Tony, on her first day of college at the age of 17 and knew the moment she met him that he was the one she was supposed to marry. She did, and they now live on 5 acres in the country with their dog Blue. They have 4 grown children and 5 grandchildren spread from Massachusetts to Southern California." What person, man or woman, would not want to be so lucky in love?

She also had an unbridled and unfulfilled passion for writing, and had aspirations from childhood. She shares, "I've always been a writer, even though it took me years to realize it. As a teenager I wrote stories in notebooks and penned poems for fun. As a young wife and mother, I spent all my free time reading romance novels, which usually meant between midnight and 2 a.m., and thinking that I could write stories like that. But as our family grew, my husband had his own dreams to pursue so I put my ideas aside and helped him as much as I could. I did write a novel in the early 90's, but that was before the Internet really got rolling and I had no idea what to do with that manuscript. I honestly believe I could have been a huge success if I'd sent it to Harlequin at that time. But I had kids heading to college and two younger ones still at home, so I filed it away."

This scenario has played out countless times before, maybe even in your life. You have, or have had, a passion for something, but for whatever reason could not pull it off. Maybe marriage or parenthood took priority. Possibly a job that paid well but left you unfulfilled. Maybe you had a spouse and kids- or even parents- that you needed to support. The reasons are many, and that is why "*Most men lead lives of quiet desperation* and go to the grave with the song still in them" according to Henry David Thoreau.

Onward with Tori's story.

In the world of romance novelists, the RWA, Romance Writers of America, is one the biggest trade organizations in that industry and *romance novels* are incredibly huge as a business. In 2010 they accounted for $1.3B in sales revenue and accounted for 13.4% of the cumulative publishing market. They exceed most other book publications including mysteries, science fiction and fantasy, as well as religion and inspirational books and according to R.R. Bowker's Books In Print, there were 9,089 romance titles out of 832,253 new titles published in 2009 and the numbers were higher in 2010.

From the RWA site, "In 2009, the best-seller lists were dominated by romance fiction titles, with 375 editions of 357 titles by 167 authors under 51 imprints on the *New York Times, Publishers Weekly,* and *USA Today* lists for the year. These numbers mean romance fiction was the number two category by a consolidated ranking of bestsellers, beat only by movie tie-in books." If you cater to the "build it and they will come" theory, then the market is ripe for more romance novelists each year.

The publishing industry, like many others, has gone and is going through many changes, especially the challenge of the e-books, i.e., books that are self-published and never go to the big publishing house. This is creating a huge drain on "conventional publishers", but opening up big opportunities for writers. Tori shares: "With the dawn of a new century (2000) I decided it was *my* time. I got on the Internet and learned about RWA, joined writing groups, went to conferences and met agents and editors. I submitted a manuscript and almost sold it. I wrote another and almost sold that. I was a finalist in the prestigious RWA Golden Heart contest and won the Colorado Gold contest. I wrote more manuscripts and finally sold one to a well-known small press publisher."

With each success sometimes comes a roadblock and that happened not long after she won the award and was devastated by the death of her father-in-law, which set her back five more years. "When my father-in-law died I had to help my husband in the business (photography) they both shared. Then the economy tanked and so did the business. We found work doing high-volume photography, but it was grueling work with long hours, little pay, and zero appreciation. I quit writing all together. We did that job for 4½ years, and I hated every minute of the last two years of it."

Since she is a terrific writer I share more of her story in her own words: "In May, 2011 my fellow writing friends spoke about how much money they were making by self-publishing their books on Amazon and Barnes and Noble. Before that, I'd turned my nose up at Indie publishing because it seemed like a cop out. Everyone wants to be published by one of the Big Six, right? *But now I was desperate to find a way out.* We'd been living below the poverty level for two years and if I could pull us out by putting my books up online, then why not try? I was expecting to make a few hundred dollars a month, but hoping for more." (When you reach that point of pain, when you can let go of your ego, you are on the path to growth.)

"I turned 57 in June (2011), and put my first book up online two weeks later and I made $60 in that first two weeks. Then I put up two more books and made $106 the next month. I added a short novella the next month and made $600. It hit number one on an Amazon best seller list and I hurried to get the sequel up. That one knocked the first one out of the number one slot and I made $4500 in November (2011), selling over 10,000 books that month. At that point I let my husband retire. In December 2011, I sold just under 30,000 books (that's 3x November), and was at the top of the best seller list and in the top 100 overall on Kindle. I earned $14,000 for the month which is more than I made in all of 2010 at my J-O-B."

The lesson to be learned here is that Tori AKA Pam had a passion for decades and had a series of starts and stops until she reached that breaking point. For many it takes that pain to motivate us to start doing what we want to or should be doing. Tori was able to exceed her income from her job, do what she loved to do, and allowed her husband to retire from something neither wanted to do and instead help her in her business.

When I posed the question, "What lessons have you learned that you would like to teach other young entrepreneurs about "success?" she responded with "The only thing holding you back from realizing a dream is *fear*. Find out what it is you love most, and find a way to make that your career. Go back and look at what you did for fun as a kid, what was your passion? Can you make a living doing something similar?" And so I ask:
"What is your passion? What is your excuse for not pursuing it?" One of the trends I see in Boomer's stories: unfulfilled dreams and desires and previously unrealized or underutilized strengths and skills. SOME are entrepreneurs, others are more creatives, but regardless of where you fall, don't just think about it: DO IT!

Are you concerned that you are too old? It is only a state of mind and if you can use your mind to accomplish those long unfulfilled dreams, then make it so. This youth-centric world does still afford opportunities for those at any age, and Tori finishes up with "Back when I was young, we didn't really look at being a success at a young age. We thought that was something you worked toward and it usually meant having a decent retirement. This was before Steve Jobs, Bill Gates, etc., and since that time the mass media and public sometimes are too fixated on age."
To reach Tori: (www.toriscott.blogspot.com, toriscott@gmail.com):

If you find yourself asking yourself
(and your friends)

'Am I **Really**

a writer? Am I

REALLY an artist?'

Chances are

you are.

The counterfeit innovator is
wildly self.confident.

The real one

is scared
to
death.

* Steven Pressfield 'the War of Art'

(13) Creative Boomers, and patterns emerge: Pablo Solomon

Can you imagine a sculptor, an artist, who goes by the name of Albert Solomon? Not to sound biased or discriminatory, but a highly ethnic name like Albert

Solomon puts in most persons' minds a picture of a businessman or an accountant or something along those lines. And that was just one of the reasons that Albert, called Pablo as a nickname at an early age, decided that as his creative career became more significant in his life, a name that he could brand would be a wise move. We'll get to that point shortly.

Pablo is 64 now and always had a knack for art, which presented itself in the form of dance, drawing, sculpting- and martial arts, which is how he made his living starting at age 12. As a young skinny child raised in the tough neighborhoods of Houston, Albert had his share of challenges, many of which were overcome by education, something his parents stressed at an early age. Since he was constantly bullied they thought it wise to try martial arts- jujitsu specifically- partially to give him greater confidence and secondly, to defend himself in case he got into trouble. And he excelled. Man, did he excel, to the point that when he was 15 he was practicing many hours each day and involved with tournaments. In addition to jujitsu he also trained in other disciplines and in his words, "What tied everything together was Kali--Philippine knife fighting- which gave me a way to tie in the other arts in a systematized manner which I could teach specialized units." He maintains that regiment of physical conditioning to this day and at the "ripe old age" of 51 he taught classes for the Queen's Guard in the Netherlands. "Since discipline was one of the core tenets of martial arts, he decided after graduation to focus his life on his arts and opened a studio. Meanwhile he went on to college at the same time, got his degree in three years and went on to get advanced degrees, though rarely a part of his profession.

He grew his business to three studios and then in the eighties the recession hit Houston like a brick. The oil industry was devastated and though he wasn't in it, the ripples affected him regardless. He downsized his three studios to just one and kept that going for some time, yet always had his eyes open for other opportunities. In speaking with this man that gets up every morning between 3:00-4:00 am, his energy literally vibrates through the phone, so you can imagine the energy and focus he had thirty year ago. He had some successes buying and selling antiques, furnishing cafes, exercise studios, and board and breakfasts, but his heart and soul remained in the creative fields, especially dance. Alongside his martial arts studio he did some counseling and teaching and got married at age 30 to wife, Beverly, who remains the love of his life. "My partner is my wife who is my muse, and she does most of the actual business and keeps me from pissing off clients," Pablo confides, spoken like a true "artist!" His wife was and continues to be a big supporter and introduced him to a friend of hers, Marilyn, who encouraged him to truly, really, with 100% determination pursue his artistic mission and to find a way to position himself as unique and a brand in itself.

With help from his wife they opened a studio and with the newly found power of the Internet in the late 90's found other artists that he wished to work with. Pablo's particular strengths are in the stone and clay medium, but he works in others and starts most projects with his greatest strength- his drawing skills. His studio in Texas carries his creations as well as others he admires and though he doesn't get mind blowing dollars for his work, "most of them sell for an average of $5,000 with his most expensive piece selling for $25,000." As a martial artist and dancer he maintains a focus on doing drawings and sculpting of dancers, many famous ones and others not so famous. It is a niche that works well for him since he has the background and connections and personal appreciation of the human form. He was a founding teacher at the Houston Contemporary Dance Theater in the 70's, so this was also part of his "branding," as his wife's friend Marilyn suggested.

Promotion does not happen in a vacuum and Pablo shares: "I started building relationships with writers, photographers and publishers which has resulted in me being profiled in 23 books, most of the major magazines and newspapers (from Wall Street Journal to National Geographic), on national TV, doing promotions for PBS, on international radio and even being subject of a short film that aired on HBO." That is good promotion for anyone.

"Art really is a matter of confidence," he says. "You either believe in yourself or you don't. Most of the great artists were megalomaniacs or committed suicide. Rothko was a good example of a great artist who never could get over his self destructive mindset. On the other side of the coin, Bernini and Caravaggio had no self esteem problems--- violent tempers, but not lacking in confidence." One of the great things I enjoyed in our conversation was his candor about money. Many "creatives" as I call them and artists of many sorts believe that they need to live like the stereotypical "starving artist." When I posed the question, "What advice would you have for those that really DO wish to profit from their talents?" he said, "Too many artists want the fruits of capitalism while living anti-capitalist lifestyles. Art is a business and you must approach it that way. There is no greater freedom than economic freedom in a free society." Touché'

Many in the arts have the "starving artist" mindset and believe that selling their product is a "sell out" or "cop out" of some kind. I personally don't get it but I'm glad that

Pablo understands that you need to make a living to continue creating. I asked him about retirement and he laughed, since that word is not even in his vocabulary. "Many great artists live to a very advanced age," he says. Picasso died at age 91, meanwhile marrying a much younger women and it seems the creative talents bring an inner peace of mind and is something that can be carried on in many cases until the century mark. "State of mind is vital and it's important to be around the right people," he shared. "As the Boomers age, many want to fulfill their life long dreams of being artists and writers. I am inundated with people my age who want to know how to become a successful artist. Of course they want it overnight with some sort of magic and not hard work, discipline and tenacity." Even though this book is about Overnight Successes, that success can take many decades to evolve, but that's OK. The fun should be in the journey, not just the outcome!

To reach Pablo: (www.pablosolomon.com)

life is a great
big canvas,
and you should
throw all the paint
you can on it.
-Danny Kaye

(14) Hattie: a Cougar's cougar!

Is it possible to re-invent yourself at age 75- as a sex expert? Hattie (no last name) believes so and has positioned herself as an expert on cougars, defined as "older women who date younger men."

She didn't start out that way but actually owns a company that teaches holistic health and beauty tips. Always a sleek and attractive woman, Hattie was a model for Dolce and Gabbana when she was in her seventies and her goal was always to show that the body is attractive- at any age- and sexual activity should continue as long as our hearts are beating. Hattie's take on the impact she has made: "I'm pleased to be on the front lines of this sexual revolution. More and more older women are dropping their shame about being sexual (and their underwear too!). They're shortening their skirts, flaunting their cleavage, and loving their mature bodies."

But interestingly enough it's not just the older gray hairs that appreciate and respect her; the younger people do, too. Continually she gets e-mails and hugs on the street of those who recognize her familiar face and she is even asked for autographs, calling her the "Old Lady Gaga!" Hard to believe you can become a pin-up senior citizen poster girl at age 75, but the goal of finding fulfillment at the later stage - or any stage- is to find a need- *and fill it*. There seems to be one here as every day there are over 10,000 Baby Boomers hitting age 65 according to the US Census Bureau and that will continue until 2030. If we push that number out even further- to age 100- according to the AARP, American Association of Retired Persons, there are about 7000 people hitting the century mark each day. Can they-do they- should they continual sexual activity? That is a rousing YES in Hattie's camp.

Hattie has gotten more than her share of publicity and notoriety, appearing on the Howard Stern radio show first in 2000 and again in 2010. At her first go round she was warned that Howard might make her feel uncomfortable and make her say something she didn't mean to say, but Hattie turned the tables on him. Always appropriate Howard called her a "hag" (he was 47 at the time, Hattie was 64) and said he would never sleep with anyone that old. She came back with "This old hag sleeps with men who are MUCH YOUNGER than you, Howard!" Then he called out several twenty-something aged guys on his crew and asked them if they would screw me. They all answered that "they would in a minute." To add a topping to that statement she pulled off her top and went bare-chested the balance of the interview and the show was so popular it was repeated several times.

Ten year later, in 2010, she was invited back to Howard's show and even though she did not go topless when asked if she would do it again, Hattie shares that "I would do it again in a minute."

Life has given Hattie her share of challenges, including heath issues, when she developed Fibromyalgia in 2003. Fibromyalgia is a medical condition with no identifiable cause and includes such symptoms as long-term, body-wide pain and tenderness in the joints, muscles, tendons, and other soft tissues. Fibromyalgia has also been linked to fatigue, sleep problems, headaches, depression, and anxiety. Considering that she was an active woman and taught other how to do likewise in her career as a Movement Therapist, this was a major setback and forced her to stop working. She had written some books on aging, but that was not profitable enough for her to live comfortably.

One day in 2010, out of the blue, she answered an ad on a web site called Help a Reporter Out (HARO), which is a bulletin board for connecting the media with experts in certain areas. She responded to a search for an expert on "Cougars" which in turn led to a major television appearance on the Learning Channel for a show called "Strange Sex: Cougars and Cubs." That exposure allowed her to begin a private practice as a Holistic Life Coach specializing in Anti-Aging and Sexuality. Since then she has been invited to appear or be interviewed on many other shows, including CBS News... twice.

As of this interview she is focusing once again on writing her story, a book about her "unusual style of aging exquisitely" along with developing a speaking career on the same subject. You can be sure you will see her on TV again and she continually promotes herself to various women talk shows. Her goal is to "inspire others to claim and manifest their dreams... at every age." Her main lesson is about becoming UNSTOPPABLE and shows how she turned her personal health issues into something positive. One of her mottos: "Impossible = I'm possible!"

At any age we can and do feel discouraged and feel that no matter how hard we push and try, it will not work; Hattie, and others like her, are the reason for this book. Age is not a barrier; just a measuring mark. As Hattie says, "When I need to take a break, I do, and then I go back with a renewed energy, hope- and commitment."

As I looked for those to interview for this project, those at *any* stage, I asked for people that have "made it" especially pertaining to financial success. But "Making It" is a state of mind. We must all experience ourselves as "making it" by our own definitions and that means having faith and courage and resilience.

Hattie's info: (www.holisticallyhattie.com, hattie@hattieretroage.com)

> "Age is not important – unless you're a wine"
> Anon

(15) Gary Foreman, a Boomer embracing technology

For someone in Phase Three mode, can you start an on-line or web based businesses without having a background in that field? Is it possible to develop an exit strategy if you know you may be terminated from your job? Of course the answer is yes, and Gary Foreman is a case in point.

Gary spent most of his life as an employee, but had a dream to do his own thing. Now age 59, in 1995 Gary and his wife started "The Dollar Stretcher" web site, publishers of newsletters, articles and a website dedicated to helping people to "live better...for less" as their slogan suggests. Gary shares, "This business is a third career for me, but it incorporates not only pieces of the previous two careers, but also skills learned away from work," which perfectly identifies WHY having a business and having success in Phase III is not that difficult IF you look inside yourself and look objectively at your passions and your experience. He was in his young forties when he started The Dollar Stretcher and there is no way he could have had decades of experience- and failures- to look back on, unless he started this project when he did. Is he making a fortune in his business? Has he "made it?" According to Gary, "I think that as we get older we tend to define 'success' a little differently, so our incentives would be different, too. Younger people are more likely to be very committed to making a lot of money or becoming famous. Somewhat single minded. Older people tend to be a little more balanced in their view of success." True enough all across the Boomer board. But on top of that he loves what he does, sees no retirement in his future, and takes pleasure in knowing he is providing valuable information to help his followers. Like many of our stories, Gary also got his college degree, acknowledging that it offers little help now, but recalls that he got into college with a Debating scholarship. That helps in his conversations and public appearances and especially allows him comfort during interviews on the radio and other web sites. His actually degree is in Business Management which is a good background as he manages a staff of four.

As a lifelong entrepreneur I believe that small start-ups and on-going businesses like The Dollar Stretcher will create more jobs individually than most "major manufactures" that are re-hiring or hiring new personnel. Can you help yourself; help others and help the overall economy, too??

Gary also has a practical take on success and what it means and why not everyone will become successful in their lives. As many struggle today I asked him if he had any advice that he learned along the way. "First rule, make sure that you're not stubbornly pursuing something that cannot happen. If that's not the case, then keep trying. Too many people fail because they quit just a short time before they would be successful." And though success is good and success is fun and you can profit from it, it may not be the keys to happiness for everyone. I asked if he encourages other "older" entrepreneurs and provides an example for them to follow and he added, "Only if they want me to. I'm willing to encourage people if they want encouragement, but if they're happy with life it's not my job to make them unhappy with their existence or tell them what could make them happy."

Putting this model of e-commerce into perspective, if you are at your Third Phase in life and have an affinity for computers and would like to do something a bit more "clean" and high tech, then you should look into e-commerce. How big is this field that increases almost 20% every year? According to invesp.com, in 2010 it was a half a TRILLION dollar business and by 2015 it will be three times larger. Past numbers and projections according to the web site:

2011 $680 billion
2012 $820 billion
2013 $963 billion
2014 $1.2 trillion
2015 $1.5 trillion

If you build it, will they come? Only if there is a real advantage or saving to the consumer, either in money or in time, or both. Here are some of the top reasons that we shop on-line:

73%   save time. That speaks for itself. In just minutes you can buy on-line- and research first- what might have taken you hours to locate and purchase years ago.

67%   more variety. There are few absolutes in this world but the one thing you can be 100% sure of is that no store in the world could compete with the selection and variety of on-line stores. The 800-pound gorilla in this fight is Amazon.com which sells almost half a million products *each day*. Some items they inventory, most they fulfill from third parties (on-demand), and in addition they have sites that they manage, plus their own on-line auction. If a building was large enough to physically stock everything they had it would be the size of a state!

59% it's so easy to comparison shop. I can recall the times when I would go to several stores with stock numbers in hand and compare apples with apples. We will never need to do that again. Ever.

58% it's less crowded; that's me. Not to be sexist or biased but to many women shopping is a sport; a social gathering. For men it can be an onerous chore. Give me what I want, let me pay, and let me get back to what I was doing!

55% Prices are cheap. With limited inventory, focused employees and the ability to outsource much, there is no brick & mortar business that could compete with an e-store unless they were selling a loss leader just to bring activity.

40% less gas. Actually no gas. With gasoline prices as insane they have been over the past decades, e-commerce is one of the wisest and most frugal moves you can make.

30% Less taxes, and in some cases, no taxes. Depending upon your state it is possible to save state taxes if you purchase from outside your state. As of this writing that advantage is in flux and even though the on-line seller may not charge you tax, your state may insist (?) that you calculate and pay it anyway.

I recall seeing my first computer in 1979 when I worked at a car dealership. The finance manager put a contract in a dot matrix (you remember those, right?) printer, and on screen was that contract in digital form. Of course I didn't know the word "digital" back then; it was just "there." He plugged in the numbers on the screen and 'poof', out came the forms with the right numbers in the right place. Just three years later IBM had the vision and mission to put one of these boxes on everyone's desk and many scoffed.

We've come a long way since those early years, and 1979 was considered the genesis of on-line selling via an Englishman man named Michael Aldrich. An inventor, engineer and entrepreneur Michael spent years in the early versions of IT (Information Technology) and worked for large names such as Honeywell and Burroughs. His creation was primitive and slow and few used it, but this was 15 years before Tim Berners-Lee "invented" the World Wide Web (protocol), followed my Netscape browsing and many, many more in the following years.

The transitional year was 1995 as Amazon was launched, initially exclusively as a seller of books and later of everything else you could possibly want or need, followed shortly thereafter by E-bay. These two concepts were the "killer apps" as they used to call the BIG innovators or game changers in the technology world, and made their developers and many of their staff extremely wealthy.

Do you have a killer app in you? In today's world you don't need to invent one, you just need to _find_ _one_ and apply it in ways that help people or relive their pain or gives them what they want. Oh yea, the other thing you can absolutely 100% count on? E-commerce will never, ever be smaller than it is today and will continue to dominate commerce worldwide. As the Far East leads the world in technology savvy youths, and mobile technology (look at the Smart Phone in your hand) becomes part of everyone's lives, e-commerce will be as natural as dialing a phone number and completing a call.

"You are never too old to set another goal or to dream a new dream..."

- C. S. Lewis

(16) A healthy-minded celebrity is born: Stephanie Mansour

How does a young girl, not long out of college, get on television and became a local and regional celebrity with something as commonplace as personal training? Oh, and it's taken just four years. Really the question is, "Can anyone (including you) do such a thing and become well known and successful in just a few short years?" Stephanie is 26 now and even though this book is focused on Baby Boomers and those over 50, there are many lessons to be learned from the younger generation. Not all of them are tech geniuses and able to become wealthy at a young age writing software or developing on-line games. Many of them do it in fields that are available to *many of us.*

She went to college at the University of Michigan which was close to her roots in the upper region of the country. For those that went to college you may recall this phenomenon called the "Freshman 15." That number may be random and somewhat arbitrary, but the term is not. Per Wikipedia it describes the weight gain that many new college freshmen put on in their first year in college. "The purported causes of this weight gain are increased alcohol intake and the consumption of fat and carbohydrate-rich and more fast food in university dormitories. Many dining halls in United States universities are all-you-can-eat style and offer copious dessert choices. In addition, lack of sleep may lead to overeating and weight gain." That is the official description but the two biggest factors are the ones that are some of the benefits of going to college: freedom to indulge- in food, alcohol, partying, and sleepovers, and generally a lack of focus on academics with a strong focus on slacking. The Freshman 15 typically describes the weight gain by the females since the guys for the most part don't care as much and are not as perceptive or caring of their appearances.

Stephanie caught that weight gain bug and saw others around her with the same problem so she decided to go to the campus TV station and suggested they offer a TV exercise show for the students. They loved the idea and asked if she would host it. Since she was always athletic and had a love of exercise she decided to take the challenge. "Victory favors the Bold," and the show was a hit and became popular and even won the title of Best New Show on Campus. She wasn't shy, but this was well outside her comfort level, so she faced the challenge much like she faces all challenges, head on with grit and determination. "Take risks and trust yourself," was one of the comments she added in the questionnaire I used with all my profiles. So after doing her show throughout college she knew this was her goal; to get her own exercise and fitness show. Being a role model forced her to some degree to live the lifestyle that she purported to teach, which was actually a good thing for her own health. She majored in Communications, which of all the people I interviewed, is one of the few majors that actually related to her chosen career. She took many classes in Women's Studies and Psychology, so when she graduated she had all the academic credentials to make her dream come alive. One of the additional things she did was pitch the college TV station to give her her own women-centric talk show for the female persuasion, which they did and she hosted for a year.

Now it was time for a Reality Check- the real world of entrepreneurialism. As anyone that has been self-employed knows, having that degree and those academic credentials can only take you so far and from what I have seen in my consulting career, many business owners know what they know, but not what they do. Immediately after graduation she focused on getting into television, but she knew she did not want to be a reporter or anchor or someone along those lines, but instead wanted to learn it from the inside, the behind the scenes. Since she was in Chicago she went right to the top; the Oprah Show and Dr. Phil Shows and Lifetime television (Television for Women) and succeeded in getting a job at Lifetime where she worked for a year. Shortly after she did get the call from Dr. Phil's Show and got hired there to help in the creation of new concepts department which required her to move to the West Coast, so off to California for another year of learning about TV behind the scenes. She got to know the persons behind the scenes as well as the guests and became a sounding board for many, all of which confirmed in her mind that her own TV show was the destiny she wanted to create.

.

She knew after a year it was time to create her own life so it was back to the Midwest and time to start making her own living and she focused on some of her core strengths, which were yoga, Pilates, personal training and body image and confidence coaching for women. She knew her market, targeted them and went on to build a business. Like most businesses it started slow and grew, from about $25,000 gross income her first year to a healthy six figures just two years later. Naming her business "Step It Up with Steph," she also decided on a color theme, one that resonates with women and remains consistent in her marketing and that is her choice of hot pink as a color theme. Going back to her "take risks and trust yourself" attitude she overcame many friend's and counselor's suggestions.

"So many people told me Step It Up with Steph and hot pink were horrible foundations for a business, but I'm very glad I stuck to what I wanted." It is not always easy to stick with our convictions and decisions, but gut feelings are right more than not. She also started her business for the right reason which was to truly help others. Money was always in her mind, but the "give first" attitude drove her as it does many other successful business owners. Of the many things she did right, she created pre-paid exercise packages which allowed her to get commitments and a degree of dependable income. Initially fearful of selling her $4,000 packages, she found that there was an audience. *All she had to do was ask.*

Recalling my days when I started in real estate I remember how difficult it was to get "older clients" to trust you, and Stephanie ran into similar obstacles. For the most part age is a state of mind, so regardless of your age and for Stephanie it was an easy fix. She shared, "I've been told that I'm a 40 year old in a 20-something body. Some women older than me question how I can really help them with their bodies – but when they give me a chance, they see how mature I really am." The proof is always determined by the results so if you are 25 or 55, do not let chronology determine your commitment or level of success.

Since she began her business her income has doubled and she has been profiled on many media channels including CNN, AOL, Yahoo!, WGN TV, Crain's Business, and TV stations across the country for her holistic and unique approach to being healthy and fit anywhere, anytime. Her "Cubicle Crunch" is a series of exercises for office workers to do in their free moments to relieve stress and get a quick stretch. She created a workbook, "30 Days to Love Your Body & Your Life" and is now ready for her next stepping stone: her own TV fitness show. Her web site has many video segments from various TV shows where she has appeared and her engaging personality and comfort on camera offer a huge advantage. She looks the part and she believes in herself and what she does. They add up to success. What I found particularly revealing about her business model was that she is focused on becoming a "brand", someone that can sell things, without investing her personal time in creating, which is very smart. Many trainers or sales person or anyone that profits from their "own efforts" is limited by the hours in a day. Stephanie developed a line of exercises, videos and books and sees herself helping those with health problems on television. Considering she did all this in just four years is impressive and a great inspiration for any of us at any age.

Stephanie's info: (www.StepItUpwithSteph.com, Steph@StepItUpwithSteph.com)

Let's revisit once again the different Generations and how they are defined:

❧ Generational Overview: ❧

Baby Boomers: born 1946-1964 (Phase III)
Massive numbers, massive influence, but are their best days behind them?
The numbers: about 73 million.

Gen X: 1965-1980 (Phase II)
Children of Boomers, in many cases SET in their ways and integrated in jobs they cannot or will not leave- until (unless?) they are forced to. Smaller than the Boomers in number with **46 million members**

Gen Y: 1981-2000, (Millennials, Phase I) The Digital Generation, mostly under 30 and huge in numbers and potential influence: **about 80 million.**

(17) Phil Johnson: an Inevitable Success

Can you, by sheer force of will, learn to be successful? The answer is yes, of course, since success, by whatever definition, *is* determined by *sheer force of will* and attaining it is an internal decision. What is success? For the purpose of this book it's about financial success, which may sound shallow, and even vague, since we learn to live off what we make. Others define success by state of mind and peace of mind and having a comfortable life. Those are also true. So the question comes up, "How does a 15 year old boy will himself to be successful?" If we get to know Phil Johnson of Master of Business Leadership in Toronto, Canada, we have a great example of that.

Phil is 58 years old now and hails out of Toronto, Canada. He has developed a business leadership program that he trains on worldwide with offices in the United States as well as several foreign countries. He lives comfortably now, but had a difficult time in his early years. As I have researched this book and interviewed dozens of persons I have found that many of them come from less than ideal circumstances. So the question about "force of will" and self determination is not rhetoric or high concept marketing. They are real forces and we should investigate how they present themselves.

His story is so encouraging and motivating I would rather share his words: "I was born in Brantford, Ontario, Canada in 1953 and lived in a small two bedroom bungalow where my mom and dad raised three boys. I am the youngest and was a surprise as my mother was in her mid 40's when I was born. I was born six weeks prematurely and weighing just four pounds and spent my first six months in an incubator at the hospital. Later it was discovered that I was born with dyslexia, a neurological disorder, which causes my mind to re-arrange numbers and words. It makes reading and working with numbers very difficult and I did not even realize I had the condition until about 20 years ago. In school I was labeled a "slow learner," and prayed that the teacher would not ask me a question.

I started working at age nine, pulling copper wire out of the back of dumpsters and selling it for five cents a pound. That was my "allowance." My mother died when I was 14 from breast cancer and went through radiation, chemotherapy and ultimately a radical mastectomy. One month after she died I made a decision that was to change my life.

I made a conscious decision to help myself and help my friends that had already given up on life. From then on I became an "A" student, and my Dad died just a few years later. I graduated in the top of my class at McMaster University in Electrical Engineering and began 25 year career in the semiconductor industry. The company where I worked grew to $1 Billion in annual sales and I traveled almost 60,000 miles per year. Before I hit 40 I was living in a beautiful house with a pool near Toronto, Ontario and my career was on the rise with several vice presidential roles. Yet I asked myself and one of my older brothers and queried: "Is this all there is?" I accomplished more than I, or anyone else, ever thought I would and yet I was surprised that I felt less than fulfilled and not very happy. And I was disappointed at the quality of the leadership and emotional intelligence I had experienced in my life and about this time remembered the promise I had made to myself in January, 1968 about helping kids who had already given up on life." This "crossroad" of life and questioning is prevalent through all the generations at certain points.

Pretty powerful and compelling story and one that emulates many others like Phil. So what is success? Is it just money? Just a nice house or car? Can you be a success and be broke? I think the answer falls in between and we all must fulfill our own definition of success. This book is about "overnight success" but rarely does it come overnight. In this time warp we call life, overnight can happen in a very short while or it can take decades.

As a trainer and speaker Phil offers some of his experiences as "chapters" which in his case he breaks down into three: the first half, halftime, and the second half. For Phil the half time came as he reached that epiphany that begged him to ask "Is that all there is?" and he was in half-time mode for 11 years. A long time.

During that time he reflected on his life, what he did, and more important, what he did not do. His dyslexia, which he considered a curse in his youth, gave him an exceptionally clear mind to focus on specific tasks at hand which preceded developing the MBL Leadership System. He reflected over his past 20 years and more than 50,000 hours of study, research and "in the trenches" consulting and coaching experience. In the last 10 years he has worked with organizations and individuals primarily in North America using the MBL system to develop authentic leaders and organizations with emotional intelligence that are capable of obtaining the results they want with less effort and more fun.

Even though Phil is a businessman- a successful one at that- he thinks conceptually, too and of the power of the universe. "The development of a clear, passionate Vision enables us to move from success to success or failure without loss of enthusiasm," he shares. "We each have an unconscious set of habits and beliefs that reflect our "winning strategy" for achieving success. **We** did not design our winning strategy; it designed us, and is the source of both our success and our limitations and defines our reality, our way of being and our way of thinking. It focuses our attention and shapes our actions, determines what is possible and what is impossible. Our winning strategy is not what we do; it is the source of what we do."

Do we have to ask if Phil has found peace; found success and is now complete in his life as he carries on the third chapter? I believe this answers reflect all that and more. In closing I found a great quote from Phil's new book, "The New Economic Currency": "Water will never boil at 211 degrees F; its "escape velocity" is 212 degrees F." The simple message is that the diffeerence between being static and elevating yourself can be as simple as One Degree.
Phil's contact info: (www.MasterofBusinessLeadership.com, mblcoach@masterofbusinessleadership.com)

DON'T BELIEVE EVERYTHING YOU THINK

(18) Andrew Schrage: Gen Y Aggregator Extraordinaire

From the many interviews for this book, one fact was very evident: you do not need to create content or material to become successful. Some times you can become an aggregator, or compiler or even a broker of the widgets or information that you sell. That opens up huge possibilities since many times we feel we are not qualified to offer X, Y or Z, *but* if you can find those developers of X, Y or Z and be the conduit, then you can create a successful business model. It does not matter if you are 65 years old, or 25 years old, like Andrew Schrage. Andrew is a perfect example of the new entrepreneurial Generation Y business owner. The ones that are not satisfied with the status quo or working with others and the ones that want to have a *life* in addition to a career.

Andrew was fortunate in his life with two respects; one was that he had a father that was an accomplished and successful business person and had a background in investment analysis and high-end money management. This is a very specialized area and one where you gain a unique internal view and understanding of money. Surely not everyone with that experience knows how to use it or benefit from it, but for Andrew it gave him a financial sense and literacy at a young age. He is actually one of the few I spoke with that went to college and graduated in the same field which he chose to pursue, and that was a degree in Economics from Brown University, one of the most prestigious Ivy League schools in the country, located in Rhode Island. No one goes to a school of this caliber on a whim or without a sense of what they expect to do afterwards. At least we hope not. Andrew also went into the investment field after graduation, but it did not stick and he explored ways to take more control over his life.

The other benefit Andrew got was the support of his parents that encouraged him to take risks and to not follow the status quo. "My parents were very influential in encouraging me to do what I was passionate about, even if it meant taking bigger risks and giving up a full-time income as a result," shares Andrew and that support cannot be overstated. When you have the support of someone that believes in you it increases the likelihood of success significantly. Spouses, mothers, fathers, siblings or even friends; having a support staff that encourages you to find your own success can be a game changer. As I discovered in others for this book, the "failure is not an option" attitude is the rule, not the exception. None of these successful entrepreneurs got there "the easy way" and even if they are "there" that is no guarantee of future success. This whole success path is a journey and it is very easy to get sidetracked and even defeated after you have made it, as we saw with Timothy Sykes who did go off track. Andrew carries that same message with observing, "If I and my business were to fail, I would pick myself up, dust myself off, and start over learning from these experiences."

His business- his web site- (www.MoneyCrashers.com) is a compilation of articles and guidance on smart money management and much more. It has some similarities to Gary Foreman's "Dollar Stretcher" business, but each has a different model and focus. Andrew's site is attractive, easy to navigate and unlike many similar sites, is very user friendly and not intimating. Many that have financial services sites veer off course in two major areas. They are either too robust or complex for the "average person" or they are too heavy on sales or advertising which makes it intrusive. Fortunately Andrew avoided both those pitfalls. With articles as diverse as "Extreme Couponing" to "18 great uses for WD-40" to "Ten reasons you should study abroad in college", Andrew's site has about 10,000 registered subscribers and is free. His monetization is exclusively banner and advertising sales and he has the support of major players like Chase, American Express,

Visa and MasterCard as clients. That is very impressive and the obvious reason for those advertisers to stay with the site is because they believe the audiences' eyeballs fits their demographics. They must since these advertisers remain.

Andrew works from home- the cheapest location if you can pull it off- and has one partner his age and about 30 "team members" nationwide that provide content. Some are paid and others are not, which gives an aggregator like Andrew lots of flexibility with monitoring his cash flow. Working from home, aside from being cheap, also offers another advantage and that is the fact that if you *can* work from home, you can probably work anywhere. Welcome to the world of mobile officing to the max.

"There is an entrepreneur in all of us, " Andrew says, "and the ones that take advantage of their talents and turn them into money-making opportunities are the ones that will benefit the most both personally and financially. It can be extremely rewarding to go the entrepreneurial route." His major function within his six-figure revenue generating company is to provide Search Engine (SEO) exposure and to write some content. The web site has been featured and provided content for many high profile media sources, including USA Today, the Wall Street Journal, MSNBC and Forbes.

As a point to note: If YOU, the reader, are not computer savvy or have a full understanding of the value and opportunities of the Internet or on-line marketing or SEO, DO NOT let that stop you! Those with that knowledge and insight are everywhere- and for an affordable price. You do not need deep pockets to start a company or web sites like this- you just need to be unique and distinctive. There are a multitude of ways to collaborate or partner with those with specialized skills or to develop affiliate or associate programs to allow everyone to work with you in your business.

I asked Andrew where he wants to take his company; his long term vision. He acknowledges "There is really nothing new or unique in what we are doing. We'd like to expand our offering into other forms of media, like Podcasting or video." At the age of 25 and with his singular vision I think his likelihood for success- by any definition- is very good. Can a web site like this make you rich; a millionaire? The answer is YES, it can. The more visible players, the Googles and Facebooks and Twitters of the world all do the same thing; they bring subscribers and a loyal audience to the advertisers that want to sell them stuff. Andrew has 10,000 subscribers, some of them buying from his advertisers. If he has 10 million subscribers will he get more advertisers paying more money? This is the mindset that all Baby Boomers should focus on if they want to go into an on-line type business. To reach Andrew: (www.moneycrashers.com, andrew@moneycrashers.com)

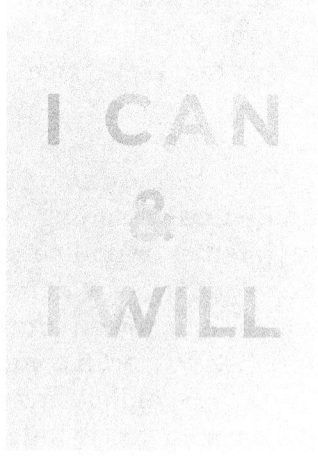

I CAN
&
I WILL

(19) The Brilliance of a Crazy Idea and the Craziness of a Brilliant One: Boomer Craig Wolfe

Ducks. Rubber ducks. Rubber *collectible* ducks. Would anyone in their wildest imagination ever think you could create a million dollar business with rubber ducks that can be personalized to look like celebrities, sports personalities, mascots from colleges, or icons of products on the open market? No, virtually no one in their right mind would ever try such a thing, which makes it evident that you do not necessarily need to be in your right mind to create a successful venture! Sometimes you can be off the wall and abstract and totally bizarre and create a fortune. Need I remind you of the most famous money making idea of 1975: The Pet Rock? Hold that thought, we'll revisit that in a moment

Craig Wolfe's journey was one of the most intriguing I heard of all the persons that shared their stories. Like many of us "Children of the Sixties" we transitioned into adulthood without a lot of direction and thought that Love really *was* all you needed. Many went to college but really tried to avoid "selling out" or focusing on a career. Craig graduated with a degree in Business and Religion, but had no idea what to do with that. In his words: "I really had no direction. I always found that if I wasn't moved to something emotionally, then I couldn't really conceive of it as an area of serious livelihood for myself. Many of us lived in an idealized world thinking that war was bad, money wasn't important and living for the day was the cool attitude to take."

For those of us in the Boomer age bracket like Craig, age 59, we were the first generation raised on television. And cartoons! The Golden Age of cartoons in the sixties had great stars like Bugs Bunny and Daffy Duck and his

Warner Brothers and Looney Toons cronies, along with Fred Flintstone teaching us the past and the Jetsons the future. Yogi Bear, Mr. Magoo, Rocky & Bullwinkle, Underdog; they were iconic and since we generally had less than half a dozen TV stations to choose from, we were their captive audiences. Google "cartoons from the 60's" and you can get your dose of nostalgia via Youtube. We had no idea how cartoons were made and no one understood that there was money and opportunity in such simple creations. Until Craig had his epiphany in his early twenties as he walked into a store and saw an original "cel" drawing of Mickey Mouse from when he first appeared forty years earlier. And it was for sale! WHAT?! You can buy these things? He had no idea and most of the world didn't either.

"I was instantly captivated by the raw energy in the animator's hand drawing." Craig shared. "It was one of the actual drawings that was used in a real 1930's Disney cartoon short. I had no idea that people could own these things or that they even existed. Finally I had some direction: I would seek out places to get more of these "cel" things and thus my original business **Name That Toon** was born with the plan to buy and sell original Disney vintage animation drawings. "Icons of happiness" is what he calls them. For reference sake, "cel" is short for "celluloid", which is a transparent piece of plastic (highly flammable!) that was used for animated drawings. They were used up until the early 90's until the more efficient and less expensive digital recreation became more effective.

As the saying goes, "We don't know what we have till it's gone" and that is very true of our youth and desire for nostalgia. Every generation for the past 100 years longs for those "good old days" and typically they revisit their youth in books, (comic or otherwise) or cars or paintings, but now we could own our cartoon buddies. Revolutionary, insightful, and brilliant. What better way to create a business than to relive your youth and help others do likewise?

Name that Toon did not become an overnight success, but Craig had fun. One of the tenets of business is "find a need and fill it", but the problem here was that there was no need, and there was no market until Craig created one. It was close to the surface, he just had to uncover the top surface. Challenging? You bet. His imagination went wild as he sought out other types of nostalgia including one that everyone knows about and pre-dates cartoons even further: Coke. The drink, not the drug. Craig continued his story: "One day I saw in a window all these old vintage Coca-Cola vending machines, old glass bottles of Coke, and other assorted memorabilia. I was dumbstruck. In an instant I felt all the power of those old time commercials, vending machines, all the feelings of nostalgia and old time feelings of time past. I immediately went inside and worked out a deal to buy their whole window display. You can see how it dovetails into the cartoon cel business, too. Now he's expanding the lines and offering other items that people might want to display and collect. Many would stop there, but when we're young we don't know what the world may deem impossible, so Craig contacted Coca-Cola corporate and in a year's worth of negotiating and compromise was able to license many of their drawings for reproduction. A coup, as they say in French. Technology was advancing and many of Coke's television characters were not drawn on cels anymore, but were created digitally. These were paradigm changing worlds and decades ago computers were readily available to government, Big Business, and those with deep pockets, and Coke has always been known for their innovation. The success with Coke led to licensing agreements with Anheuser-Bush, M & M candies (talk about extremes!) and especially the California Raisins

The California Raisins were a great example of how the California Raisin Advisory developed such a powerful ad campaign and created caricatures out of raisins. 'Anthropomorphism' is what it's called and it can be used to create a human-type "character" out of anything. Cartoons are a great example as well as talking Geckos and other noteworthy ads. The Raisins actually were not animated, but instead were "claymation" which involved creating a clay character and making it move millimeter by millimeter, frame by frame, to create the look of motion. It is time consuming and the master of that game is Will Vinton who created TV shows and movies featuring clay characters. The Raisins were so popular that they even aired a Primetime TV Special called "Meet the Raisins" which was a bio-type show about how the Raisins became famous. That required giving them names, histories, personalities and singing voices, all because an advertising agency told the Raisin Advisory that raisins singing "I Heard it through the Grapevine" would make raisins sell better. Plus Marvin would be proud. They were right and it allowed merchandising to many outside companies, including Craig, who sold many of the animation cels they created along with other memorabilia. Craig also became close friends with Will Vinton which was another perk of selling his creations as well as Art Clokey, the "father" of Gumby. Craig did likewise with many icons in the animation field and developed strong relationships with Warner Brothers, Disney Studios, and many of the famous creators behind the product. If success can be rated by the strength of your contact list, Craig was reaching some lofty levels.

The story could end here, but our focus is on reinventing and finding new markets, so in 1998 Craig realized that his plan was flawed; he owned nothing outright, just licensing rights to someone else's creations. Many would say "who cares?", but Craig wanted his own "thing", so in his late forties he sold off his company and started making ducks. Rubber collectible ducks. Made to look like people, both famous and real and some that were fictional. CelebriDucks since then has created rubber ducks for the NBA, Major League Baseball, the NHL, NASCAR, NCAA Collegiate Mascots, and also celebrities and musical groups such as KISS, James Brown, The Blues Brothers, Charlie Chaplin, Mr. T, Shakespeare, Barack Obama, and many others.

This business model actually started as a fluke. From Craig's web site: "My daughter, Rebecca, a product design major, designed the entire line in the beginning. When the Philadelphia 76ers read about us, they asked us if we could create a rubber duck of superstar Allen Iverson complete with tattoos, cornrows, and earring for a stadium give-a-way. It came out extremely well and I would always joke that our rubber duckie looked more like him than he did! After the 76ers event took place, we began to receive a great deal of national and international attention." Success is when preparedness meets opportunity and that led to many others both in the sports world and the business world. The CelebriDucks were used as promos for major league sporting events and have been sponsored by companies such as Reebok, Dr. Pepper, Gatorade, AOL/TimeWarner, Southwest Airlines, Arby's, Adidas, Mountain Dew, Chevrolet, Sprite, Dodge, Clarinex, Suburu, Pepsi, Office Depot, Toyota, Sierra Mist, and many others. They have been profiled on all the major networks, plus CBS Evening Magazine, CNN, ESPN, TNT, VH1, A&E, Who Wants To Be A Millionaire, along with

Sports Illustrated, U.S. News & World Report, N.Y. Times, USA Today, LA Times, Maxim, S.F. Chronicle, Chicago Sun Times, Playboy, and Fortune. Per the web site: "ESPN ran a poll on their website for the fan's favorite stadium give-a-way and CelebriDucks won, beating out Bobbleheads, Beanie Babies, Pez Dispensers, Lunch Boxes, and Match Box Cars."

Craig did more things right than not and when I asked him what lessons "older" entrepreneurs might learn from his experiences he stated, "Don't try to be all things to all people; find your special niche and stick with it. And have patience, all good things happen in time, and remember; it's not how much money you make; its how much you keep....overhead has destroyed more businesses than you could ever imagine. Failure has created all my successes," he adds, and that is the proper way to look at success: it's just part of the learning process.

Craig has a very low overhead and virtually all his business production is outsourced to others, which keeps his employee costs to a minimum. He acknowledges that his company has been scoped out for purchase by larger ones and they all think that Craig is doing much more volume than what they really are. By a factor as great as ten in some cases. And before I finish Craig's story you should know that he has not been sitting on his rubber duckies doing nothing and has created yet another duck-centric line--- of chocolates.

Rather than repeat what Craig said, here is the genesis of this even more exotic idea: "Not too long ago we contacted Hershey's Chocolate about doing a Hershey Kiss rubber duck- a little yellow duck popping out of foil and holding Hershey Kisses. Everyone there loved it from the head of licensing to the buyer for all the Hershey stores. It seemed like a home run, but at the last minute, the brand manager for Kisses didn't give his final approval. Seems he didn't quite understand the rubber duck concept. It was so bizarre and disappointing since everyone else really loved it. Anyway, I *interpreted all of this as a sign that rather than accept defeat*, we should instead do our own chocolate themed rubber duck and our own line of chocolates." And so began Cocoa Canard, since Canard is French for duck.

"We developed this line of hand-crafted real Belgian duck chocolates to go with it and designed the box of the duck and chocolate to look like a French chocolate shop. And we came up with the idea that people could send Canard Grams to people they love; a gift of the Cocoa Canard rubber duck, the chocolates, and personalized note. And the rest just flowed."

As you may agree, Craig's story is educational since it shares some of the processes in working with Big Business, along with motivational since none of us will ever hit a home run the first time up to bat. You just have to keep swinging. The lessons to be learned are that adaptation is part of the process and you must evolve from what you are today if it is not working, or into the future when you may be forced to.

At one time the generally accepted pop theory was that it took 21 days to develop or break a habit. Whether we're referring to smoking or poor eating habits or starting an exercise program, conventional wisdom said three weeks was the template. I always took issue with that and a new study by University College of London confirmed that an average of 66 days was required for any new habits to ingrain in your mind and life. And a singular setback is *not* a deal killer or cause to quit or go back to Day One.

Adaptation can take many forms, sometimes as simple as a mind switch in your mind, other times a totally different direction in your business.

To find Craig: (www.celebriDucks.com, info@celebriducks.com)

WALK WITH THE DREAMERS, THE BELIEVERS, THE COURAGEOUS, THE CHEERFUL, THE PLANNERS, THE DOERS, THE SUCCESSFUL PEOPLE WITH THEIR HEADS IN THE CLOUDS AND THEIR FEET ON THE GROUND. LET THEIR SPIRIT IGNITE A FIRE WITHIN YOU TO LEAVE THIS WORLD BETTER THAN WHEN YOU FOUND IT.

(20) So, now, about that Pet Rock:

It almost sounds like an urban myth or fairy tale, but in 1975 the Pet Rock was born. The father of this random success was an advertising executive from Los Gatos, California who kept hearing his friends complain of how expensive and disruptive their pets were in their lives. "Who has time for feeding and brushing and taking them to the vet," they asked, so Gary Dahl decided it was time for a trouble-free, worry-free and inexpensive "pet" to own. Thus was borne the Pet Rock craze. They would never get sick or need to be fed or incur any expenses. After all, this was the Prime Time glory of the ME decade when selfish was the new norm. The idea of just a rock in a box was not going to fly, so Gary wrote the maintenance manual so the new owners would know how to care for their new found best friend.

"The Care and Training of your Pet Rock" was the piece that made this crazy idea work. The manual not only showed you how to care for your Rock, but also how to train and teach it tricks. Anyone could teach a rock to "sit" or "stand", but some tricks took more effort, like "roll over" and "fetch" or "shake hands." The one that made it fun was the ATTACK mode, which even a child could learn! Combined with this novel instructional manual was the rock, a one penny rock that Gary purchased at a local home improvement store. Add in some straw to keep your rock comfortable and some breathing holes so your rock wouldn't suffocate, and now you had something that everyone was talking about. The Rock was viral before there was such a concept, and it didn't even require a video to accomplish it.

Thinking he hit pay dirt (hmmm, maybe that would sell, too?) Gary took the Pet Rock to a gift show and Neiman-Marcus, a high end department store, ordered 500. Everyone wants to follow the leader, so the chaos ensued and the rock sold by the millions at $3.95. The rock was on the cover of Newsweek, one of the largest weekly news magazines of its day and even appeared on the Tonight Show with Johnny Carson with the "owner" joining the new Rock Star.

The Rock probably helped create more eccentric off the wall ideas than any other mainstream oddball product in history. There has never been anything like it and there may never be another. The lesson here is not in the product; it's in the lesson itself. Sometimes ideas that you think have that perfect combination of idiocy and buzz-worthy-ness can make someone lots of money. Ironically it is even easier today than ever before to create your own "virtual Pet Rock" and that is by coming up with an on-line concept that people want, or find amusing, or just plain gets them intrigued. Why not you? Why not now??

Must you be crazy to have a crazy idea? Here are a few more examples that everyone laughed at and the inventors are still laughing while counting their money:

Lucky Break Wishbone Co.
(www.luckybreakwishbone.com)
The biggest feast of the year with family and friends pigging out, and just one Thanksgiving turkey with just one wishbone? Who gets to break it and get all that wonderful good luck it brings? Even vegetarians can get their own plastic wishbone- or two- for less than a dollar apiece. Ken Ahroni came up with the idea in 1999 and a decade later they continue to sell for $3.99 for a 4-pack to $8.49 for ten. Sorry, the turkeys are not included. Their

web site even has a "call to action" in the form of a "days till Thanksgiving" countdown timer. Cute *does* sell.

Antenna Balls (www.happyballs.com)
The well-known fast food chain, Jack in the Box, may have started it, but it took an imaginative entrepreneur to monetize antenna balls. There are different companies that make the ball, mostly because it's hard to patent, but now the balls are available in any configuration you could dream of. Numbers, sports equipment (like footballs, golf & baseballs), happy (and other type) faces in every state of emotion you could imagine, letters, animals, flags and iconic images; they are available to ride on top of your antenna. They even have a magnetic version if you don't have an antenna. Like Craig at **CelebriDucks**, The Happy Ball Company has also licensed with many sports teams, both collegiate and professional. Coming up with a clever idea is just the beginning. How do you repurpose it and make money? That's where your imagination can truly fly- and profit.

Doggles (www.doggles.com)
For the animal lover that wants something more cuddly than a rock and for owners that truly believe in protective eye-care for their dog (seriously?) the Doggles are clever and surprisingly functional. Though they can be viewed as a gag, we have all seen video and pictures of dogs that stick their heads out of windows or even riding on motorcycles. These curious products straddle functionality with good humor and when you add that into the millions of dog lovers and owners out there, well, you have a money-making business. Would a dog owner spend $20 to save their Best Friend's vision? In a minute. And this company has expanded into many other product lines. After all, they have a CAPTIVE audience of dog lovers, right? Probably with a sense of humor. What else would

these dog owners buy? Doggles.com also offers mundane things like toys and collars, harnesses and backpacks, but also items that many might not think about, like floatation devices for dogs that can't quite swim. The one missing item that would put them over the top? Prescription lenses for older dogs with vision issues.

Other off the wall ideas that didn't make the list include:
- Designer Baby Bags (easy to figure out)
- Picky Domains (you pay them to come up with your web site name)
- Fitdeck (a deck of cards featuring exercise routines requiring no equipment. This is now a worldwide company doing in excess of $5M annual sales. "Fortune favors the Bold" as the Roman poet Virgil stated before Christ was born and some things never change.

And there are probably many more, enough to fill a book. Be aware that there is a very thin line between a fad, which will not last, and a novelty, which may. Coming up with a novelty that has longevity is a matter of luck, timing, and having a decent strategy to drive it.

That brings up the question of *"how do I know when I have a good idea?"* When you seek opinions and advice from family or friends, or co-workers you will get everything from "That is an awesome idea", (even as they think it sucks) to "What are you thinking, are you crazy?" when it may actually have some merit. Getting opinions from those you know well is a slippery slope and I suggest you find someone that can be brutally honest, while yet supportive. Even the Bible says, "a prophet is not accepted in his hometown" which means that brilliant people and brilliant ideas can be shunned by those closest to you.

There have been countless winning ideas that have been squashed by non-supportive spouses. What you a seeking- the ONE THING that will be invaluable to flush out your idea- is **Objectivity**.

If someone can be *objective* with you and not just say that the idea is great or lousy, but can truly dissect your concept and tell you why and how it is great or not and possibly offer suggestions, well that is a good adviser to have. I was very fortunate to have a friend that really was just an acquaintance that made this book possible.

Mike Brenhaug was someone I met several times over the years since we were in similar, pretty much competitive fields. I was a business consultant, he called himself a business coach, but we were in the same general space. He also was the president of a local chamber of commerce within a city our company wished to do business in, so we had several conversations along those lines. Mike's particular niche was teaching business persons how to Focus and avoid distractions in order to fulfill their goals. He is a staunch supporter and trainer in Goal Setting techniques and wrote a book with the title, "**WTF**." Pretty good title, right? It's called "The Interrupt" because it catches your attention: solid black cover, big bold letters with WTF across the front. It stands for "**Where's the Focus**," so get your mind out of the gutter. It also stands for "Where's the Future" and "Where's the Failure" and "Where's the Faith" along with dozens of other slogans that fit the W-T-F acronym and are inscribed across the cover. When he told me about the book and the title I thought it was brilliant since it engages the casual person with just three letters.

I went to Mike's launch of his book and he ended up selling very well over the successive months and made it to the Amazon Top Ten list. About six months after he published and as I was reaching my lowest low, I asked him to join me for coffee. I was one day away from losing my house to foreclosure and filed bankruptcy at the 11th hour; for the second time. I thought (hoped) that I had something worthwhile, but I needed to get another person's unbiased opinion. I had no health insurance (for three years), nor car insurance and felt my mortality closer than I liked.

I was curious as to how his book was selling and wanted to know if it performed as he expected and what he had learned and what would he do differently next time. Gaining the insight of someone with experience cannot be overstated and it is critical to flush out ideas, both good and bad and I told him I had a concept for a book and wanted his opinion since I knew him well enough to know that he could be--- objective. He was gracious and said "absolutely, let's meet." All I had at that time was an unproven idea so prior to our meeting I wrote up a two page overview with some possible titles and table of connects and subjects. Mike thought this was a winning subject (I hope you do, too) and he offered some suggestions on how to proceed. The rest as they say is history, but getting Mike's guidance and encouragement was a game changer for me emotionally and psychologically. HE had written his book and told me the efforts it took to do so and he said that I could do it, too and he offered to kick my ass and guide me and be my Accountability Coach. I am forever indebted to Mike Brenhaug for his friendship, his support, his guidance and most certainly for his--- objectivity. If you would like similar results his web site is: www.wheresthefocus.com.

DO NOT LET THE OPINIONS OF OTHERS CONSUME YOU

(21) "Time waits for no one, and it won't wait for me" sings Mick Jagger. The 10,000 hour Dilemma: we ain't got time for that, so how about a Two-Year Success Plan?

Dr. K. Anders Ericsson, a psych professor at Florida State University, shared the theory that to become extraordinarily successful in any field takes about 10,000 hours. Malcolm Gladwell in his book "**Outliers**" drilled that down and shared many observations that validated that number. If you look at some iconic and significant leaders in various fields he backtracked their success and came very close to that 10,000 hour mark. Cited were tech wizards like Bill Gates and Steven Jobs, along with the great Beatles rock group. It seems to go across the board from the creatives to the business leaders and one example that was highly scrutinized was the story of hockey great Wayne Gretzky, who started playing as a young child, and really came into his own at a fairly young age, but still about 10,000 hours later.

If we put that into realistic terms the question is, "How long would it take to reach the 10,000-hour mark?" If we spend an average of 40 hours per week working on our chosen target, that's about 2,000 hours a year. So it would take about five years to become a leader in your field. If we start young, like many star athletes or musical virtuosos, they can be there in their teens. Good for them, but we don't want to commit or have that kind of time. Committing 40 hours a week to something- anything- without pay or assurance of success is fine when you have time on your hands, but in today's easy to be distracted world, that is not a realistic goal for any Baby Boomer. Even if we committed 20 hours per week, that's still a 10 year target to hit your mark. Sorry, but I'd have to pass on that. And what is interesting to note is that many Gen Y entrepreneurs don't have that patience either! By utilizing technology and other resources many of them are cutting the 10,000-hour mark into shreds.

Some may be able to "master" their chosen target easier than others. For myself, I have never been or considered myself an "athlete" so any sport where I wished to excel would take much longer than some teen or twenty-something with greater concentration and hand-eye coordination. And I could practice from now till we land on Mars, but I would never be an accomplished singer that anyone would like to hear. So the 10K mark is merely a check point; a historical standard, but may not have applicability to someone just *starting* their mission. If you are in school, high school or advanced, and if you have a goal to be or do some particular thing, then allocating five to ten years to do that is fine. After all, that is the way the game has traditionally been played, right? On a recent blog I saw this comment: "As my karate teacher told me years ago, it's not practice that makes perfect, it's perfect practice that makes perfect. If you are spending 10,000 hours practicing how to do something, and you're doing it incorrectly, you'll still be bad at it 10,000 hours later. You have to spend those hours productively, practicing how to do something the right way every time." So the reality is, it is easy to practice incorrectly and waste precious time. Just as it's great to practice, it's also great to plan, but don't forget the quote from one of our greatest songwriters, John Lennon: "Life is what happens when you are making other plans."

So instead of "trying" to figure out where you want to go with your life, why don't we make it easier and quicker and hopefully less painful? Let's work on a Two-Year Success Plan. And to be clear we're talking about business success, not reaching nirvana or some altered state of consciousness. The goal here is to BECOME an "overnight success"- in two years.

If we start today and go immediately to the 24-month mark, let's work backwards. I DO NOT want to hear you say, "I'm too old" or "I can't" since this book dispels that objection. And let's be practical. Some things you probably don't want to or shouldn't or can't do:

- Rule #1: You can eliminate anything that takes athletic or artistic skill. I know there are many that have creative or physical talents and if so, maybe you can ignore this rule. But if you are 50+ and have never "made it" as an athlete or singer or dancer or ventriloquist or world class artist it is probably too late to start. The corollary would state, if you do it for FUN and a sense of accomplishment, then by all means carry on.

- Rule #2: Since education takes time and focus, both of which are less than they used to be, then skip going to college and getting your MBA. What would you do with it, get a job? The time for concepts and theory and rhetoric is behind you; now it's time for practical application and real world experience. As I stated earlier, this book is not a primer on getting a job. First off, they are tougher to get, even tougher to get when you are over 50 and in today's hyper-competitive (and low paying) world, why bother? If you want to go to school for a particular skill and use that skill to develop a business that is OK. But the time for becoming a plumber and getting a union job is behind you.

- Rule #3: Don't throw money at a project or business unless you really think it will pay off. Let's say you got a financial windfall and want to buy a business. That's OK, but be sure you go in with your eyes open and have a realistic assessment of what your end goal is all about. Don't get me wrong, if you spent your entire working life in a particular field and now want to work for yourself in that same or similar field, then go for it. The caveat is here is for someone that has never had experience owning a franchise nor has any background in fast food going out and buying one. YES, it does work with some, but the question is, "Do you have $20,000-$500,000 to buy a business?" and work as hard as necessary to make it successful?

- Rule #4: Let's have a goal within the realm of possibility. The focus of this book is to open your mind and motivate you to learn from others, but this is not Fantasyland, folks. If you are going to define success in monetary terms, let's keep our feet on earth. Can you start a business and create a $10M company in two years? Absolutely. It has been done before and will be done many times again. But, that is a big but, and it may take more money, time, commitment, skill and practical applications than you have time for now. When I use the term "overnight success" I want you to consider the goal line within reason and within sight, not half way around the world. If making $100K a year would change your life into your Golden Years, then let's use that as a target rather than making a million dollars. Maybe it might be just an extra $5,000 per month? Maybe $3,000 would change your world? I suggest you shoot for the stars and if you hit the Moon, then it's still a win.

Other than that there are no rules and it's time to find your creative gene and make something with it.

Self assessment time: What are you good at? What do you like to do or do really well?

The list of things that I do not do well is long and what I do well is shorter. For me personally:

What I do not do well	What I am good at
Hate reading contracts or boring stuff with too much detail or jargon	I recognize skills and talents in individuals and organizations that may not be connected, but could or should be
Don't like spreadsheets that make my eyes glaze over. OK in small doses	I am not a workaholic (some might argue), but if a task needs to be done, I will stay with it. After all, I wrote this book, right?
Since I have two left feet anything that involves exceptional balance or athletic ability I will pass on	Teaching and training. My ego is comfortable being in front of a group and I believe in being prepared, but can improvise pretty well.
I have patience, but only to a certain point. Don't push it.	I have good command of the English language and can write and speak good? (sp. Joke)
I play well with others, but have a tendency to think outside the box. That is great for me, but bothers	My highs are not that high and my lows are not that low. Even as a split personality Gemini my

some.	extremes are not.
I like and appreciate technology, but gave up "trying to keep up" a few years ago. Social media is great, but I dance on the surface.	

I could go on, but you should do your own. If the list of things you do well is longer than what you are poor at you may be thinking too conservatively. The good news is that what we're not good at can be filled by someone else that is. In this world of collaboration (see "good at list") it is easy to find someone that supplements or compliments your skills. Remember, "It is easy to fail alone, but it is difficult to succeed alone."

The other side of the 10,000 hour coin: As we agree that it takes 10,000 hours to become proficient at something, it also takes that amount of time to condition yourself for failure. I was listening to a radio show and the guest was saying that when he was young the words "I can't" were forbidden by his father. His Dad allowed them to say, "I don't want to," or "It will be difficult," but never say they could not do something. That conditioned his mind for much longer than 10,000 hours, but whether we like it or not, we have all been programmed to do (or not do) certain things. The environment we were raised in and the attitude of your parents are imprinted in all of us, good or bad. If we fail at things and get used to it, it sometimes takes an effort to break that pattern. If you have been conditioned to accept failure, then please stop and objectively assess if you really *failed*, or maybe you were just **unsuccessful at that time**. Success is a state of mind, failure is only temporary. By the way, that radio show guest was Phil Keoghan, the host of the CBS television show, "The Amazing Race." The contestants on the show travel around the world following clues and along the way have to do some local customs that are many times scary to them. They have to confront their fear of water, or heights and other phobias that they may have. Phil is a wonderful role model for that hosting position and lives the life of positive-ness, to the point that in his younger years he made a list of amazing things that he took on himself. Among that list is setting a world record for bungee jumping, diving in the world's longest cave and riding a bicycle 3,500 miles across the America as part of a multiple sclerosis awareness campaign which developed into a documentary called "The Ride."

As a motorcycle rider (not biker) one of the biggest dangers we face- and fear- is running off the road. Sometimes it is caused by errant drivers or obstacles or wild animals or circumstances outside our control. Unfortunately one of the biggest causes of motorcycle accidents is called "fixation" which is what happens when you focus on a particular spot- and go there. Rounding a corner on a windy road, if you fixate on the edge of the road, where do you think you will go? If you focus on what you want to achieve and where you want go the odds are you will get there 100% safely.

What a wonderful thought it is that some of the best days of our lives haven't happened yet.

(22) Bookends: the interesting relationship between Boomers and Gen Y (sorry to exclude you, Gen X)

Sometimes when you start a project you foresee certain occurrences and outcomes, but one I did not anticipate was the "relationship" between Gen Y and the Boomers. Boomers have a major drawback in trying to create QUICK business success in today's world and much of that is because of the complexity and necessity of social media and technology. I used to be proud of my ability to stay on top of things, but changes happened so quickly I fell way behind. What used to be today's cutting edge in six months becomes obsolete and when you think you have "it" down, something better comes along. As I was interviewing Phil Johnson he was sharing how the pace of technology and change is moving exponentially faster than ever before and will continue to do so.

In the world of Social Media the 800-pound gorilla is Facebook, which in just a handful of years has a greater population (over 600 million as I write this) than many countries of the world. Having a web site and a following is not nice to have anymore; it is critical to have, especially with a business. Even large companies such as Proctor & Gamble are starting to understand to the point that they are downsizing amazing and talented people and are replacing them with a handful that can duplicate the presence that the company is seeking. And many times that handful is overseas, carried out by inexpensive laborers and technicians in India and other Asian countries. The Flattening of the World as you may have heard.

In order to compete and reach success *quickly* it is critical to have an on-line presence. This includes web sites, of course, but also all the social media platforms like Facebook and the other Big Three or Four or however many there are. The list of other social media sites numbers well in to the hundreds.

Along with Facebook you have Twitter, the new Google+, LinkedIn, Pinterest, and too many more to name. Here are some interesting stats to review:

Social media site	How many users	When did it start
Deviant Art	25M	2000
Facebook	640,000,000	2004
Flickr (primarily photo sharing)	32M	2004
Google+	20M	2011
LinkedIn	100M	2003
MySpace	100M	2003
Orkut	18M	2004
StumbleUpon	10M	2001
Tumblr	13M	2007
Twitter	175M	2006

Courtesy of: www.howmanyarethere.net/how-many-social-networking-websites-are-there , www.ebizmba.com/articles/social-networking-websites, www.socialbakers.com/facebook-statistics

There are many (most) that I have never heard of and there are more users and sites outside the United States than within. Facebook has about 160 million of the 640 million worldwide users (and is declining) so that means almost half a billion others are throughout the rest of the world; there are more Facebook users in Asia than all of the United States. The ramifications are significant because that means you can *create* something- anything- and then create a worldwide presence in months. Not years, but months.

The world has changed and many Baby Boomers are seeing that but don't know how to react- or capitalize- on it. The Gen Ys do. They understand technology, have been raised in front of a keyboard (now Smart Phones) and take to this new world without a thought. I know texting for me is a pain in the ass, but Gen Ys do it effortlessly. So why not develop a collaboration between these bookend generations?

According to Google, 63% of all businesses nationwide do not have a web presence, and if I was to speculate, I bet that 90% of those without are of the Boomer Generation. A web site is not an option anymore, nor is a social media platform, yet 97% of all consumers go on-line to research and to shop. This changing paradigm creates huge barriers to Boomers growing their businesses or starting anew.

During my research I met Chris Chong who runs www.seosmartLinks.com. He is a Gen Y success story and I discovered him by accident. There are no accidents so I interviewed him and found that he was a perfect example of the *missing link between the two bookends* since he works with many Boomers and helps them market their businesses.

If you look at some of the challenges from both ends of the spectrum we already identified the challenges of Boomers to understand, embrace and utilize technology and social media. At the other end are these brilliant young Millennial minds that were working with computers while in grade school. Technology and adaptation for them is as effortless as a Boomer turns on a television (soon to be replaced) and switching or adding channels. As well as they adapt to technology they do not play well in a corporate environment in many cases and they have a huge drive to create and control their lives and their own business. They were raised with computers that allowed them to be creative, whether it was with art or spelling programs in elementary school to the evolving computers and educational requirements as they advanced. Add to that the Internet, which since 1995 (or so) has put virtually any and every fact that anyone wants at your fingertips and suddenly you find a future with no technological limitations.

I cite the example that early in my career I was investing and always needed to research companies and stocks and other financial information. It was time consuming research and involved libraries and other specialized reference sources. If I needed access to facts they were not at arm's reach and I had to find an encyclopedia or other specialized book, and then I was only able to use the latest information that my sources offered. In workshops I share the story that if I asked the question "What's the capital of Albania" (or any other country) in 1985 it could take hours to retrieve the answer. When I share this story now, the audience whips out their phones and has the answer in under a minute (Tirana). How do *I* know the answer? As fast as Google can *anticipate* what my question is, they offer an answer.

So take this generation with so much intellectual knowledge at their fingertips and hamper them with youth, inexperience and high emotional levels and it can cause failure in many forms, including the businesses they try to create. Many companies that go through this cycle and grow and perhaps get big and go public hire an experienced, mature, older CEO or CFO. Apple was a great example when they brought in John Scully in 1983 after luring him away from Pepsi at age 44. Even though his relationship with founder Steve Job was tumultuous, Scully grew the company from $800 million to a ten-fold increase to $8 billion in his decade on the job. Considering that Apple had started just seven years earlier and grew to $800 million is a great story in itself, but had they continued without executive and experienced leadership who knows where they would have ended up, but possibly not in your pocket or purse right now.

The lesson to be learned is that you do not need to be an "Apple" stature operation or even one with that design to seek the voice of experience. But if a Millennial wants to grow- or even form- a company to go from Point A to Point B, it helps to have a navigator that has been there, done that. The experience of decades is irreplaceable and many young entrepreneurs know that and the irony is, business in itself has not changed all that much. People are still people and want relationships and my belief is that there is a Matchmaking opportunity here and Chris Chong thought so, too.

Chris is a Gen Y with great technical skills, and his company helps clients create links with other possible web sites. His company name, seoSmartlinks says it all: SEO, an abbreviation for **Search Engine Optimization,** is the combination of science and art that allows your web site to be found by the millions of people that may be looking for someone like you. The whole field of SEO has become a more than $6B industry over the past decade and will exponentially grow in size with no end in sight. With billions of web sites out there, the question remains: "How do you get 'found?'" The #1 goal of everyone is to be on the #1 page of the #1 search engine, which is Google. The problem is that most SEO companies will claim to do that, most never could and most never will, but on top of that Google has gotten smarter over the years and changes the rules on a regular basis. At one point all you needed to do was have certain "key words" and "metatags" built into your site and the seekers would find you. Now the search results are determined by a very complicated and complex algorithm that reads every word of every site and looks for the most appropriate response to any specific question or search.

The world of Blogging has also dramatically changed the SEO world. Per Wikipedia, in 2011 there were 156 million blogs in circulation and that will increase exponentially from now on. Any web site of significance has a blog and many blogs are stand alone, which means that the blog is the primary offering instead of an add-on to a home page which is selling something. As we have seen from some of the stories that are shared here, the importance of blogs is significant since they are very easy to "share" and "re-tweet" in the vernacular of Facebook and Twitter. So imagine this scenario.

Scenario: You are selling your most excellent widgets, and you do everything right and create a beautiful web site. It doesn't matter how pretty it is, you could have a Mona Lisa portrait sitting in the back room, undiscovered. But let's say that someone, anyone with a blog or a following finds your most excellent widgets and writes about how great they are. Now others find out about it, too, and before you know it (ideally) you go viral and everyone knows about you. Twitter really hit it big in August, 2009 when Ashton Kutcher became the first person with One Million followers. In **March, 2011** it was reported that 366 people had more than one million followers and at that time Lady Gaga had a measly 8.7 million followed by Justin Bieber. To demonstrate show how fast things can jump, in less than one year Lady Gaga has doubled her exposure to 19 million as of **February, 2012** with Justin still lagging behind with 17 million. Ashton Kutcher has fallen to 11th place but still commands an army of 9.4 million. It is obvious that the celebrities that engage the youth will have the most followers but even President Obama carries the #12 spot with 12 million followers. You ask yourself, "so what", right? The reality is that these celebrities carry a lot of pull and are just an extreme example of the power of social media and why Boomers are missing the boat if they/ we don't know how to use it. Following the Twitter feeds in volume are the blogs and they are important since that is where Chris's business fits in. In the world of Twitter frenzy and blogging if you have something very cool that everyone loves and everyone writes about, you can become an overnight smash over night. The Twitter feeds can be sent around the world several times in a matter of minutes and your blog (or widget in this case) can be exposed to millions just as fast. If Lady Gaga loves your widget and she tells her 19 million fans you become a hot commodity. To put things in perspective, of the 242 countries in the *world* only 60 of them have a larger population than Gaga has followers. Don't forget that Rebecca Black, the young teen songwriter that everyone ragged on, got 30M views of her video, and was a guest on the Letterman Show and Leno, too. "Success can be your best revenge" aside from money, so who's laughing now??

NOTE: By the time you read this Lady Gaga will have more than 50 million Facebook followers as she just broken through the 20 million twitter followers. Way to go Gaga!

SEOsmartlinks provides content for all those channels and currently has access to over 45,000 blogs. That means with just one keystroke Chris can get someone exposed over 45,000 times. They also publish articles and provide SEO reports so you can gauge and adjust your marketing for maximum results.

What particularly impressed me about Chris is that he sees there is a market with Baby Boomers and they likewise see a market with him and he has worked with many Boomer sites not just helping them, but going the extra step and acting as a consultant. I believe that this scenario is paramount to the growth of Boomer businesses, whether they are brand new, long term or still in development. Another common bond that Boomers and Gen Y share today is "Cause Marketing" or social responsibility. In essence it is defined by those that want to "give back" which means that nonprofits and volunteerism are both targets for both ends of the generational bookends. Whereas Boomers were raised around various extremes of racism and sexism and a "mostly white" America, the Gen X and Gen Ys were surrounded by more equality than America has ever seen. Mixed race, same sex, mixed ethnicity marriages are not the exception any more and young people want and support those causes. Boomers in many cases also want to Give Back and I have seen many instances where "humanity strikes" many in their forties or fifties; sometimes beyond. It's the realization that it's not all about the "I" and recognizing the "we" and "others" is a good thing. It seems to be a byproduct of middle age and the understanding that more of your life may be behind you than before you. Finding causes and charities and churches to support becomes more significant as we age and that is one more tie that brings the two generations together. So if the Boomers need the Gen Ys technical prowess and skills, and the Millennials need the voice of experience and reason and common sense, and wrap that under a cloak of "doing the right thing", then it appears we have the makings of a great partnership. Per a 2010 Pew study report called, *Millennials: Confident. Connected. Open to Change,* Millennials were the only participants that did *not* cite work ethic as one of their top five "principal claims to distinctiveness." In this survey of about 1,200 people of all ages, the older generations cited *work ethic* among their top five choices, while the largest share of Millennial respondents said *technology use defined them.* Maybe a mutually healthy common ground would be good for all??

Chris with seosmartlinks is a fourth generation entrepreneur and his great-grandfather emigrated from Japan and later owned a chain of convenience stores in the Hawaiian Islands along with a noodle company. His father is also a business owner and Chris's decision to not finish college was a non-issue for his parents since they saw and were evidence of the benefits of hard work and an innovative mind. Chris started consulting while in college for a short while and concluded that he could and would make more money on his own and having a degree offered no benefit. This conclusion is one reached by many Millennials when they start recognizing their value in a tech hungry world that appreciates their talents. He also reached the conclusion that his biggest motivator is lifestyle- not necessarily money- as cited above by Pew. This characteristic is very prevalent among his generation as they see the generations before them work insane hours for unappreciative employers that offer no security or guarantee beyond their annual report. It's all about taking control of their jobs instead of letting their jobs control them. That does not mean you need to suffer for your lifestyle and when asked about his revenue Chris shared they are over the half million dollar mark annually. As The Duck Man, Craig Wolfe, earlier shared, if you keep your overhead under control you do not need to make a lot of money to have a comfortable lifestyle. If there is a template of a Millennial that was doing it "right" he fits into that model.

Chris has also been active in his church which he acknowledges is "multi-generational and multi-ethnic" and that church has been a great source of mentorship for him and others. He started his company in 2002, only 16 at the time and still in high school and he had the insight to create his company with partners which he still has! His recognition and appreciation of the value of the older generation and avoiding avoidable mistakes is a big contributor to the success factor of many Gen Y businesses. For a young man of 26 he also knows that the Internet really is just a tool- a mechanism- to provide quicker service and reach more people. But the other side of that coin is the human factor; the one on one relationship he strives for.

As Chris and I conversed we found a common bond and that was the desire to create a mechanism and resource to help tie the Boomers and Gen Ys together though *intentional focus* and results with Chris's amazing talents and insight. One of the biggest goals of his company- my mindset- and this book, is to create easy access and tools for the Bookend Generations. As we talked about some of his clients, and you will meet John Geffel shortly, I queried him about the successes he helped them create. He acknowledges that it took him a few years of trial and error and trying to hit an ever moving target, but now after a decade of experience he believes he has the right business model that works. The good news on top of that is that adaptation is integrated into his business plan so he knows and will go along with changes in the economy, the market place and in the world of technology. If Baby Boomers and Gen X can accept that it will be much easier riding the new waves rather than fighting them it will ensure on-going success.

```
What screws us
up most in life
is the picture
in our head of
how it is
supposed to be.
```

(23) Some things the Gen Ys have going against them

As much as they have many strengths going in, they also have some things going against them and much of that is based on being in the wrong place at the wrong time, economically speaking. As the cliché reads, "even a stopped clock is right twice a day," sometimes events just happen in your favor. What that means is that some times it is almost impossible to be wrong. The most glaring and recent example was the great timing and insight and the brilliance many American investors had in the early 2000's by buying real estate everywhere in the country, especially some of the Hot Spots like Las Vegas, Phoenix, Florida and parts of California because real estate never goes down in value. Hype and speculation created (in their minds) genius in making investing decisions. Sadly I was caught up in that, too, and lost two rentals I bought in Florida and Texas. But for years these brilliant and gutsy investors could and did make money flipping houses simply because the tide and trends were in their favor. Alas the Millennials can only vaguely recall and benefit from these past glory days, and now, as they enter and exit their twenties they are trying to compete in the toughest job market we have seen in decades, if not ever. The carnage of Speculation has left highly educated college graduates and those with advanced degrees and those that are doing the right thing as victims of the Great Recession. Many cannot find a decent job, and if they can, they do not command the salary that they would have fetched in 2005. Too many people chasing too many jobs as we face the highest unemployment levels since the Great Depression.

The highly respected Pew Research Group's survey recently showed that 41% of Americans believe that the Gen Y age group is suffering the most, followed by the

29% who think the Gen X is most damaged and coming in last with 24% who think the seniors sector is most damaged. You can be sure there is bias in all those numbers, but no one disagrees that the Millennials are getting the short end of this very small stick. Where there was more consensus is with the 69% agreeing that it is more difficult for young adults than what their parents went through to get a job, pay for college, buy a home and save for the future. For Boomers we were always told that each new generation had it better than the last and buying a house was the "American Dream" and saving for the future was easy if you started early and stayed consistent. Those lessons can be discarded as can many other rules that have been taught for decades and there are significant numbers of Millennials that have no interest in home ownership and have no faith that it is a smart investment. Rather than invest with others where they have no control, they invest in themselves. Some might view it as arrogant, but if they do it with wisdom, insight and guidance they may end up the winners in this race. The Millennials are in a quandary and truly cannot plan anything since there are more questions than answers and it is hard to gain traction or leverage. In studies prior to 2004 the Gen Y (younger sector) usually rated their quality of life on par with the Senior Sector with over 50% claiming their quality of life was "good to excellent."

There are two possible outcomes here and we may get some of both. The upside is that the Millennials have an unusually high amount of self-confidence and self-respect and remain generally upbeat about their future. They do have much to be thankful for since many were afforded the perks of the go-go late nineties to mid 2000's and had lots of high quality education, access to technology, toys and encouragement to create their own realities. That is good and much of that is fodder for the huge percentages that are starting their own businesses, sometimes by intention and sometimes by lack of alternatives. The other scenario is that some of them will have a depressed opinion for the future because of what they have seen their parents endure. Lost jobs, lost homes, lost savings and investments may cause some to maintain a Depression era mindset where they are mistrustful of banks, institutional investments and Big Business and probably government in general. That's OK; a little cynicism is good for creating a better set of balance. What would be sad is to see this generation- or the one that follows- that believes their money is only safe in mattresses and everyone in the world shuns them and doesn't care. That warped attitude can create a "lost generation" which could last *several* generations.

There is still another factor that the Millennials have going against them and if you are one, take a breath and relax cause this one may hurt. They are more spoiled than any generation before them and many of them have not been exposed to failure. They have been coddled and taught that "everyone is a winner" all through their early "T-ball" sports days through many other sports or competitive contests they ever entered. Gen Ys, the World has bad news for you: Not everyone is a winner and not every one is even eligible to *compete*!

If you want proof of this just watch an "American Idol" segment where prospective singing talents get to compete against literally hundreds of thousands of competitors nationwide. The show has been on since June, 2002 and the number of singers that have auditioned is in the millions. From those very large numbers a select view actually get on television and what is especially funny is that many of these singers believe they are really good! Some are, of course, but some have been told all their lives, "you are a good singer and don't let anyone tell you any different" so when they sing before objective judges that recognize talent, well, many times the outcome is not pretty. I am all for parental encouragement, but these Gen Ys- and younger- need a Reality Check. Over the many seasons the number one foil and the beacon of honesty was Simon Cowell. Whereas other judges would dance around the obvious, Simon would tell them, "you are horrendous," and immediately get booed by the audience behind him. So this is the unfortunate stigma and burden that many of the Millennials live under.

Many of the Gen Ys profiled here were brought up with a work hard mentality, but others have never worked in their lives before they got out of college. We have become a Coddled America where being nice to everyone and being fair to everyone has become more important than being competitive with the rest of the world. Which is why they (the rest of the world) are- and will- continue to kick our butts. If you look at the general quality and commitment for our "average" American college student and compare that with the average student in India or Japan or China, there is really no comparison. Those students are *serious* and where do they go after they get their degree in many cases? (hint: The answer is comprised of three initials starting with a "U" and ending with an "A"). If we continue down the same path we have been on we may be known as the country with a "Mediocre Society," all the more reason that bringing that hunger and experience in the Boomers together with the techno savvy of the Millennials helps us create an Above Average chance of success.

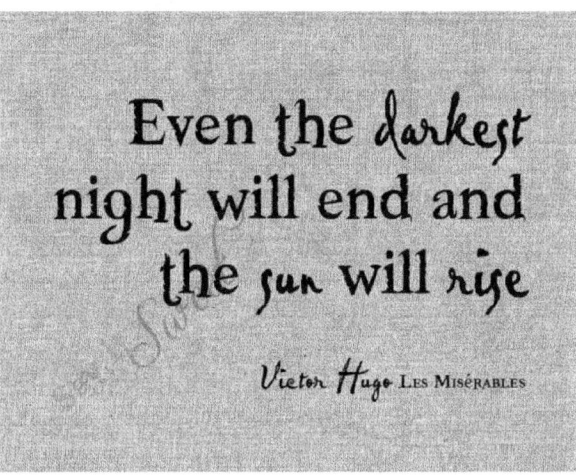

Even the *darkest* night will end and the *sun* will *rise*

Victor Hugo LES MISÉRABLES

(24) John Geffel: a Company Man ready to reinvent his life (and he didn't even know it)

I was introduced to John via Chris Chong since Chris helped John with his new company and their marketing plan. When I started this project I was specifically looking for Boomers or others that have "made it" after years of struggle and I expected to find a high percentage of entrepreneurs and self-employed persons, but I also expected to find more Company Men than I did. I thought there may have been a big selection of those that worked their way up the corporate ladder and finally, after years or decades of promotion after promotion were highly compensated and happy with job security to boot. I'm beginning to think that scenario is bordering extinction. So I was happy to meet John since he was (past tense) a company man who started right out of college and worked his way up the ladders of several companies, including two that were nationally known- and then two years ago got fired. At the age of 57. Before you feel bad for him you should know that he is happy, healthy, and is in the best position he has been in during the last 30 years.

A momentary time out to ask the question: "What would you do in that situation?" How would you react? There are two basic (very basic) mindsets for most business people: those that work for others and those that can't- or won't-work for others. Throughout this treatise the "entrepreneur" term comes up and how do you define someone of that ilk? Are they "Born that way" to quote Lady Gaga, or can they be made? Or is there an irrational risk Red Flag that cautions people of the unknown? The reality is, there are variations of answers and sometimes you are forced- **FORCED!**- to find something inside you that you may have never had to look for or find, before.

In 1978 a book was written by a Conservative Jewish rabbi that asked the question, "Why do bad things happen to good people?" and the reality is Bad Things happen to Good, Bad, Men, Women, Asians, Blacks, Whites, Young and Old. The rabbi wrote it to address his young son's death at age 14- from old age. His son was born with progeria, a rare genetic disease that causes premature aging, killing most children before they reached their teens. No one is immune from illness or failure or accidents or bad shit confronting them, but everyone handles it differently. Not that I'm religious, which I'm not, but I am spiritual and I believe things happen at just the right time for just the right reasons. Most everyone reading this has been fired or made a bad financial move or had their heart broken at some time. Free Will has its pros and cons, but sometimes what appears to be bad, turns out to be really good in hindsight.

Back to John's story.

In 1982 John went to work for Timberline, a nationally known project management software company. John's responsibility was in the marketing department, which was a new step for Timberline, and John shares, "Most of their employees were either in tech or administration, so hiring a marketing person was a new direction for them." During the early two thousands John was getting restless and started to question whether he was still on the right career path. Fortunately for him in 2006 his company was acquired by Sage, an international company based in the United Kingdom.

Newly motivated and stimulated John was ready for new challenges, and the event that opened up even more possibilities was the resignation of John's boss who recommended him for that soon to be vacant position as general manager. That new-found luster wore off fairly soon, but what turned his life upside down was a trip to Nicaragua with his daughter and their church. He always wanted to "give back" somehow and the satisfaction he got by helping to build homes and churches in an impoverished country was more gratifying than he expected. He was perplexed by his emotions and later that year went back again for trip number two. That sealed the deal. "It affected me in ways I could not imagine," he says. "For weeks I never once thought about work or checked my Blackberry for messages. I went on many great vacations over the years, but my work was never far behind. This experience I was not used to."

When he got back to the office he knew his days were numbered and he had to get out and felt himself disengaging from his new position. Considering the merger and his new obligations they all taxed his stress level, but he could not give his company all his attention. This went on for another year or so until his decision was made for him: he was laid off. He saw the writing on the wall and we have seen this story many times before with various endings. Here was a man in his mid-fifties that always had a job and now had none. That problem alone can cause issues since many men equate their actual identity and who they are with what they do and who they work for. Surprisingly he felt a sense of relief; he did not freak out and had no regrets or concerns and knew that the answer would present itself. His strong religious background offered him some stability as did his wife of thirty plus years and a comfortable monthly overhead and a moderate severance package. His kids were done with college, he had a positive outlook, but still he asked himself, "Now what?"

He didn't rush out and take whatever job he could (which many do if it is offered) and for months just relaxed and cleared his mind. Sometimes doing nothing is the right thing to do and he got some direction with a former coworker that had left the company prior to John. He was attending a leadership training class at Hudson Institute in Santa Barbara, California and invited John to join him. "It was a three day executive coaching class that conducted small group training with like-minded people, about ten per group, and challenged them with problems. We did extensive training as part of this 'Life Launch' program so the group I was with I really clicked with." One of the common bonds in John's group was their sense of spirituality so this just intensified as they all worked together, and he reflected on all he had been going through since visiting Central America with his church. After the three days were done he came out with a new set of friends and some solid answers to "Now what?" His choices were to start a consulting practice utilizing his knowledge from decades in the field, or possibly finding another similar position (quickly eliminated) or maybe work with a nonprofit since his sense of giving back was higher than ever before.

There's an old Buddhist saying that states, "When the student is ready, the master appears," and John ended up with not just one master, but many. He spent more hours at his church and also volunteered to work with an Angel investor group and helped to cultivate new start up companies and find new talent. "Over the next several months I expanded my immediate network more than ever before. I read dozens of business plans and got to know others that helped find the best ones and helped the new companies get started." He ended up meeting hundreds of people and with some of them started his consulting company called Value Driven Group. They offer guidance and support for new companies and with the new relationships he found, they were off to a great start.

One of the new start ups that was seeking help was run by a father that wanted to create a succession plan for his son and John was an integral part of that transition. That gave him satisfaction he had not experienced before and realized that working with companies owned by younger parties (Gen Y-ers) was a talent he could offer. That is how he met Chris Chong. He was more content than he had ever been in all his employee years, but the ending here is even better. He was making less money, spending more time with his church and had a great sense of satisfaction. He spoke with his church leaders and asked if there were any paid positions within the church that John might be good for. A year earlier they had offered him a position- which he declined- because the time was not right, he was not ready and the job description didn't quite fit his needs. Things were different now and John was more ready and the church had changed the job to make the fit even better. Coincidence? Maybe, but the truth is, most things happen at just the right time and even bad things can lead to better things later on. His new position also involved some pastorly functions, which scared John initially, but he expanded to become comfortable in those shoes. A win-win arrangement in anyone's book.

When I spoke to John about sharing his story for the book he thought that it might not fit since my primary focus was on becoming an overnight success after years of trying, and even though that is usually defined by monetary rewards, it still applies in John's situation. It took him 30 years to get to the place he was at right now, and when I asked him how he defined success since apparently he had found it, he concluded with, "Success to me means being exactly where you want to be, need to be and are at peace. Some times you have to let go to get there." Scott Hermann, a graphics designer friend of mine, artist for this book cover, and devout Christian offers, "Once you see the truth you cannot go back." I agree with both these conclusions and could not have said it any better.

> *"I have learned that faith means trusting in advance what will only make sense in reverse."*
>
> Philip Yancey

(25) Where does Religion or Spirituality figure in to all of this??

The answer is, it really doesn't- but it should. I was born Jewish, and baptized as a Christian in 1981, but I am not a church-goer and believe in my heart that I have a good relationship with God. You may be a follower of organized religion or a follower of the Law of Attraction, or neither, but for anyone that scoffs I can say with 100% certainty in my heart that there *is* a Power of the Universe and everything happens for a reason. My brushes with fame and failure are soon to be shared, but when it comes to Divine Providence and putting everything into the hands of a higher power, well, there needs to be some Accountability, too. Prayers are great, but your efforts will go a long way towards making them come true. Many put their faith in their own Higher Power or deity and wait for that to present itself and fix things. The truth is, it will only be available as you are able to receive it and act on it. Speaking for myself, even though I was never lazy or waited for things to come to me, many others are, or they are hampered by fear. So, some lessons I would like to share.

The term "Guardian Angel" may sound hokie, but others fervently believe that they have one. I never thought much about it one way or the other, but I have zero doubts that I have one watching over me. My Mother always said that I should be mindful and respectful of my Guardian Angel, but I was dismissive about it. She died at age 90 in 2009 on Christmas Eve Day and her last 18 months were spent in a nursing home. It was a nice place, but no matter how good they are, it is a tough place to live. I visited regularly and she always asked how I was doing and I usually lied and said I was fine. Always a chronic worrier, I saw no sense in adding more to her burden. She always said that I had an

Angel watching over me and after she passed I have no doubt in my mind she took over that responsibility and has been keeping an eye on me ever since. There is no way I should have avoided loosing my home to foreclosure after 36 months of not making payment and there were many times I was totally out of money and escaped having a utility turned off on the final day. I tried not to borrow any money, but two wonderful friends and my stepson lent me $500 during some critical times. I had no checking accounts or credit cards for two years, nor any money to pay bills, so every month was stressful, but some way, some how my Angel came through. The fact that I am still here in a somewhat healthy state of mind can only be attributed to the unconditional support of my Mother, both while alive and deceased. So Thank You, Mom.

You may have your own personal tale and your own personal relationship with your deity of choice. I believe that to be a healthy way to live and the only caveat is to remember the Greek saying that reminds you that "God helps those that help themselves."

(26) My brushes with success and failure

I once had a friend tell me about a wealthy and older client that never drove himself anywhere, but he had a nice Town Car and a driver. The gentleman always instructed his driver to park in a location where they could only move forward and never have the need to back up. My friend asked his client why he did this, thinking it might have been a superstition he had, but that was not the case. The gentleman explained, "I live with no regrets in my life and never think about what I could have or should have done; never look back and never regret, and by not backing up the car I am constantly reminded to always move forward."

I love the symbolism of that movement and wish I could be as strong in my own head. In the words of the great Frank Sinatra who did things "My Way", he sings "Regrets, I've had a few, but then again, too few to mention." I appreciate Old Blue Eye's position and only wish my regrets were too few to mention. Many times I looked back and recreated the past and the bad moves and fell back on the should have, & could have & would have, the holy trilogy of negative thinking and thinking in the past.

When I was young I was as idealistic (read stupid) as they come and never really thought too much of the future except in my very vivid imagination. I left my hometown in Pennsylvania when I was 21 and drove across the U.S. solo to California. I had never camped or cooked or had been west of the state, but I was ready for adventure. I had no career direction, no desire for school and was as footloose and fancy free as the year 1975 would allow me. And I had that state of mind for the next five years until I got my California real estate license in 1980. During those early years I traveled (again) across the country- solo- and spent a little over a year in Daytona Beach, Florida. *That* was a fun place in 1977 and I was in the car business and was able to work at the Daytona Beach Racetrack for the 500 and the 24 hour race. I met a girl (you heard this before??) in Daytona- she lived in Ontario, Canada- and I spent that summer up there and came back for the last time to California via the Trans Canada Highway. So this was my third 3000+ mile trip in three years but this time I brought a buddy with me. We only knew we were heading to Southern California since he had a friend in Orange County and would be able to crash with him for a while. We had no idea of what we would do, but he wanted to get a bar tending education and I was able to fall back on some past skills to get a job. I did that for two years and then moved to Central California and just plain kicked back until maturity finally hit me at age 26 and I decided it was time to formulate *some* type of plan.

My friend Rob remained in Orange County and after loving and leaving bar tending he got his real estate license. Timing is everything and during the late seventies in California real estate was BOOMING and he did very well. He accumulated four houses, had a nice lifestyle and then my Green Eyed Monster- envy- reared its ugly head, and I decided I wanted my own California Dream, too. I followed his lead, got my license and moved back to Orange County ready to take it by storm! The imagination and vision of a still naïve 26 year old is fun to look back on in hindsight, but frustrating to live through. My lofty plan was to work two or three years, make huge dollars and move back to Central Cal, but this time timing kicked my butt and by the time I entered the fight the Prime Rate was 20.5% and the market evaporated like water on a hot skillet. What looked like bad news at first was actually a great education since it taught me to survive an incredibly

difficult market and I did whatever my broker told me to do. Meanwhile buddy Rob and most of his fellow realtors that lived high for several years before lost most of their properties since they were all highly leveraged and dropping in value. Imagine the real estate market in 2010 and you get an idea of what it was like. Again- timing.
Over the next thirty years I did the following:

- Became a Financial Planner, got my securities license and took classes to become a Certified Financial Planner (CFP)

- When the State of California started their lottery in 1984 I saw a chance to help the lottery winners with their tax, investment and estate planning and formed Windfall Asset Management with an attorney and CPA. It was a full service shop for recipients of any windfall which never went anywhere.

- Tried more than ten different network marketing companies over the next two decades and failed at them all and spent way too much money and energy.

- One of them was a diet cookie that suppressed the appetite and allowed you to lose weight very quickly. It was actually very tasty and some people were making insane money so I used my creative mind and developed a 30 minute TV infomercial on the cookie. How much money I lost is embarrassing so I plead the Fifth.

- One of my few smart moves was forming Pre-foreclosure Specialists in 1992 since I saw the lousy real estate market returning from my earlier years in real estate. Study history, right? I was one of the first persons to structure a turn-key short sale program for banks to avoid foreclosure frenzy and contacted over 500 banks throughout the state. I met with several, they thought I was crazy and was summarily dismissed. I was too far ahead of my time. The good part was that it became a great marketing angle and separated me from most of my competition. I solicited high end buyers and sellers and made more money in one quarter than I made the prior year. The problem was that I abandoned the concept way too soon and could have ridden that pony another two years had I stuck with it. You see I met a crook...

- And started a company with him to provide document imaging for the many businesses that were outgrowing their file space and wanted to go paperless. In my defense I did not know my partner was a crook until he started doing crooked and questionable things and I thought he was smart and I was not. Seems he *was* a crook and I was beyond naïve. Some times there is but a slim line between genius and insanity and he stepped over that line and ended up in prison. The result was a great education from the School of Hard Knocks, a waste of two years and bankruptcy number one. Ironically the concept of paperless offices was a great one, but trying to sell that in 1995 was a no go.

- After all these years trying to do "my own thing"- and failing- I thought I'd get a job for the first time in 17 years. I wanted security and no risk, and that lasted about two years when my secure job and secure employer self destructed. The good news is that I learned the mortgage business on someone else's dime which gave me an incentive to do my own thing. One. More. Time.

When I say this book was written by a loser I think you can see that it was not just a ploy to get your sympathy. I screwed up more than any person at any age should have and paid the price. What I had was lots of enthusiasm, optimism and energy, but I was lacking in smarts and mentorship. I hope I can teach you from my evil ways. To say I was getting a reputation as a loose cannon is pretty accurate and many of my friends that I did not see for a while would always start out by asking, "So what are you up to now?" And I always had something.

Finally after all these experiences I was beginning to get some sense of business and I started a mortgage company and worked from home. That started well and stayed very well for about five years and I made better money than I had ever made before. Some of my failures did teach me some smart lessons and I was fortunate on two fronts. One was that I was introduced to some innovative cash flow management techniques from overseas and by following these techniques homeowners were usually able to eliminate their mortgages and all debts in less than ten years. It was legit, not rocket science, just innovative outside the box thinking. I was a wonderful master but a poor student and my Mortgage Accelerator PLUS (MAP) program was a great way to be distinctive in the competitive mortgage market. I developed a nationwide reputation in this field and it incentivized me to start a weekly radio show which lasted almost seven years until that market dried up. My golden years were fun; I was significant, deeply in debt and thought the game would go on forever. I thought I had finally MADE IT at the age of fifty-something and the MAP program was a Golden Ticket.

My radio show and mortgage partner had a great reputation and we were finally ready to hit pay dirt. One of the largest lenders in the United States was introduced to the MAP program and wanted to license it from us. That would involve sharing MY BABY with potentially tens or hundreds of thousands of users and teaching them smart money management. We thought (and hoped) that we would become millionaires during this process. Negotiations ensued and were prolonged as they usually are with a big company and then the bottom fell out. The bottom actually started to fall out in 2007 and by 2008 the writing was on the wall that was crumbling one brick at a time. It was also the beginning of the end for our private labeling with our new and prospective banking partner since they were in trouble like every other bank out there.

So in 2008 I had to figure out what to do with the rest of my life. Everything I had practiced over the prior thirty years; real estate, financial services, mortgages, the radio show, they all meant nothing and I had nothing to show for it. For the next three years I worked as a partner with a company that offered training to support cities throughout Southern California. I became their community development director and also manned our division that worked with nonprofits. I got a great education; met some wonderful people and then the recession just kept on going and finally burst my bubble. I don't regret a day of it and am constantly reaffirmed that everything happens for a reason at the right time.

During this period I became convinced that economic development *could not* be legislated or mandated by government, but had to start at the grass roots level. I created a workshop called "How your Small Business can save America." and did that in partnership with several organizations. I worked with the SBA- Small Business Administration- and ran a focus group geared towards local success, did workshops with SCORE, which is under the SBA umbrella, tried to work with the SBDC Network, which stands for Small Business Development Center, also run under the SBA and got no traction. In my partnership with OPIS Network we developed a program called "helping 100 businesses for 100 days" which was a free workshop we provided for cities to allow them to show support and offer training for their business community. The cities did not pay us, we did it to stimulate local growth and our conviction was "One Business at a Time; One City at a Time." For the most part we were ignored by cities, and shunned by chambers of commerce and were not able to make a dent in the mindset of the leaders. As I wrote this book part of the motivation was the frustration I encountered over the last three years and I decided if the Leaders won't Lead, let the People Lead themselves- One at a Time. And you are seeing part of that in this book.

but as for me,
i will always
have hope.

{psalm 71:14}

(27) On fear, ego, and appreciation for what we have

When I started to (finally) write this book I questioned whether I had enough to share. At about 100 pages my fear was lessened and at 150 pages it was like a fire hose that would not turn off! If you are afraid to try something new, to venture into unknown territory, that is OK. If your ego is stopping you because you are too set in your ways, that is an easy fix if you choose it to be. I gave up my ego and pride several years ago along with my rental in Florida, my rental in Texas, my two Maui timeshares and my motorcycle. When you truly realize that the material things that we strive for are really false evidence of success, it makes it easier to focus on regaining that success mindset. I had a friend jokingly ask me, "So when the book becomes a best seller will you remember the 'little people'" and I thought it funny. There are no little people and everyone plays a part in one way or the other. When you lose your Pride and your Ego you gain a respect for Humbleness. And if I am blessed with financial rewards I will cherish it and appreciate it like I never did before. This book opened a flood of possibilities and actually created a conduit for a sequel and several related books along similar lines. The (good) Pandora's Box I opened to authorship can never be closed.

As you can see, I collect a lot of inspirational quotes and sayings and they are peppered throughout the book. One of the recent ones I found speaks to those of us that have a creative desire and are fearful of carrying it out. Steven Pressfield in his book, "The War of Art: Break Through the Blocks and Win your Inner Creative Battles", writes "If you find yourself asking yourself (and your friends), "Am I really a writer? Am I really an artist?" chances are you are. The counterfeit innovator is wildly self-confident. The real one is scared to death." If you are or were scared to death to delve into this arena, please allow me to lead you since I was (and still am) scared to death and have no idea if my words will have any effect.

I had an interesting conversation with one of my longest time friends about two years ago when I was in a very bad state of mind. My friend Harold and I have known each other for over thirty years and when I started in real estate he had already been in the business for several years. He had his share of wins and his shares of loses and in the early nineties he, too, went through a very bad spell. He was faced with an IRS tax lien of significance, lost his home to foreclosure and like someone with my recent mindset he asked himself, "Am I worth more dead than alive?" Reminds you of George Bailey in the Christmas classic movie, "It's a Wonderful Life," doesn't it? When Harold reached his lows he told me he pulled out of it by recognizing all the things he had, instead of all the things he lost or never had and as he shared this with me it shifted my mind immediately. Once I started to appreciate what I had, especially my health, I realized that money is only transitional and it can come and it can go. He never knew that his conversation with me may have saved my life. I can only pass on that same sentiment.

When my Mom passed in December, 2009 I appreciated that she was not in pain or suffering and I was there with her, as she would have wanted me to be. I appreciated all the wonderful friends she had over the years, Bobbie Kauffman in Pennsylvania who watched over her while I was exploring my youthful trips across the country and Debbie O'Donnell who became a surrogate daughter for her while I was busy being a workaholic. My Mom became a nanny to dozens of kids when she moved to California in 1982 and I am thankful that they gave her the unconditional love only children can offer since I had none of my own.

As I drive my 10 year old Lexus that uses much more oil than it should, I have learned to appreciate the fact that I *have* a car- a nice car—and that I don't have to live in it. Control the envy and remain humble.

Sometimes you just gotta suck it up and remember that there are people who have it worse than you.

(28) Accelerating a business overnight

The title of the book reflects "overnight success" but for the most part it takes time to become successful overnight. But there are situations where you truly can go from obscurity to stardom within a remarkably short period of time. Decades ago the world and the wheels of business moved quickly, but not at break-neck speed like today. Today things move faster than ever before and overnight is not just a saying- but can truly become a reality. It can also work against you. One instance of bad press or publicity and you can become a failing company just as quickly.

For every Justin Bieber that creates a Youtube video, gets "discovered" by one of the biggest music producers in the world named "Usher" (ask your grandkids, they'll tell you) and in just a few years becomes a multimillionaire and heartthrob, there are scores of others that never see the light of day. The phenom of the moment is Jeremy Lin, an Asian-American basketball player with the New York Knicks who just recently ignited his team to a seven game winning steak, a winning attitude and created an uproar in the city and amongst basketball fans everywhere. He was not a top recruit out of college and actually graduated from Harvard, a great school for higher education, but not on the radar of basketball scouts. He created a fervor not just because of what he did, but because of what he did not do. He was waived (unsigned) by the Golden State Warriors and the Houston Rockets and was picked up by New York for an affordable $762,000 salary, which is very small by sports standards. Now he is the Toast of the Town and on everyone's lips and you can be sure his next salary negotiations will be much more lucrative than the last. If we look back on the 10,000 hour rule, you can be sure he put in his 10,000 hours to become as good as he is and the irony is that he is not at his athletic peak yet and will only get better. Some may foolishly envy someone like him that truly *do* deserve recognition and success and become an epitome of Overnight Success. Will history prove that Justin Bieber is warranted his stardom? Only time will tell.

Some ways for you to rocket yourself or your business to stardom:

- get a celebrity endorsement or testimonial

- get on television or profiled on the news. The wider the coverage, the bigger the bump. And if you are on American Idol, or The Voice, or The X factor or America's Got Talent or any one of the many reality show competitions, that can flip the coin literally and figuratively over night.

- get a cash infusion via an Angel, Venture (vulture?) Capitalist or Investor

I hate to admit it, but I am a TV junkie and always have been. I was raised on television and it was my companion as an only child. I wish I could say I only watch cultured shows on PBS and such, but I like my share of pulp and one of them is called Shark Tank.

(29) Can an 8 year old girl change destiny?? Can your life change in 14:32?

Sometimes that 8 year old girl- it this case your daughter- can ignite a spark that has been dormant for over 30 years. And some times you can create a new life and a new hope in less than 15 minutes. I wanted to leave you with a real-life fairy tale since we all need that dream and that hope that some dreams do come true.

Travis Perry is 50 years old and since he's been eight years old he's loved music and played the guitar. He was born "in the country", on a farm in Alabama and lived the life we rarely see anymore. As a child he was up at 4:30 a.m., worked on the farm and took care of the cattle along with the crops they raised, both corn and peanuts. After doing his chores, it was shower, breakfast and off to school and later in the day, after school, more chores. This might be an extreme example, but for the most part the Baby Boomer were raised in different times and learned the value of hard work early on. It is still intact today, but the pattern did not continue as strongly with Generations X and Y.

His mother was musically talented and taught Travis the guitar, which he loved, and also piano, which he hated. His mother taught him to appreciate the music and the pleasure it offered, but his piano teacher was all about technique and structure. "It was hard trying to teach an artist how to be a technician when I just wanted to learn the artistry," he shared. Regardless, he stuck with the guitar, played all through school, played in church and even with the Future Farmers of America, where he and some friends formed the group 'Silverado' that was well known. After graduation it was off to college, but his Dad's rules were very strict and he told Travis he would cover the schooling, but not personal expenses. Travis wasn't too concerned since working for a living was ingrained in his being and while in college he found a local music shop and asked to be a teacher there. That was a great fit but after about four months he was beginning to doubt his abilities since so many of his students started with good intentions and quit after about 60 days. When he shared his doubts with the owner he was told what he was witnessing the "60-day hump." Since the guitar is considered the second most difficult instrument to play (behind the violin) the retention of students is historically bad and most drop out after two months of trying. Students get sore fingers, have no calluses and lots of frustration inside, and Travis wondered if there was some thing, some device that could be attached to the neck of the guitar to speed up the learning process and to relieve some of the pressure on the fingers. He continued to teach there and that idea never left his mind since the same 60-day cycle repeated over and over.

After college he bought a restaurant from his Dad, continued to play with a group and in 1994 moved to Dothan, a small town of about 140,000 people in the southeast corner of Alabama, less than 20 miles from both

Georgia and Florida. He started a real estate and mortgage company which grew to include 25 agents and life was good. Until 2007. For those with short memories the real estate and mortgage market virtually disappeared overnight and he lost his agents to larger companies, yet continued to run his own business for about another year. "I stayed about a year too long," he confided, "and I lost everything we had, which was substantial." On a personal note I can relate after going through the identical downward cycle.

Of the businesses he retained, he kept a small bluegrass, banjo and guitar store, so with a lack of options decided that he would go back to teaching guitar even after decades of not instructing at all. The timing was right since his main instructor was looking to retire, so Travis became a full time instructor and had a decent clientele of 70-100 students per week. Within months the Curse of the 60-day Hump reared its head and Travis was amazed. "In almost 30 years, nothing had changed!" he exclaimed. "Students came in excited and in two months left dejected." That troubled him greatly, but it was his eight year-old daughter, Bradi, that turned the tide of his destiny. As a fan of Taylor Swift, a young female musician and guitar player, Bradi wanted to learn one of her songs and Travis was proud to pass on the guitar skills to her. She tried her best and one day cried to Dad "I want to quit! My fingers hurt and this is too hard," and as much as Travis wanted to see her succeed, he knew her pain and frustration was real. He went back in his mind to the idea he had decades earlier of some type of device that can be placed on the neck of the guitar to ease the finger pressure and make it easier and shared his idea with his daughter. She was ecstatic! And the words that changed Travis and his family's destiny came out of that eight year old girl: **"Daddy, if you invent it I promise to learn how to play."**

Every inventor; every artist, every creative person out there, and especially writers, have those moments of inspiration that trigger an action, but there is not much stronger than the love and trust of a pleading little girl! So Travis started to research to see if anyone- ANYONE- had come up with anything after all these years, and the answer was "no", no one had. There was one product that was close, but it was a *cheating* device; Travis wanted a *teaching* device. He wanted something that allowed learning at an independent pace and have a device that could be gradually removed from each string, one at a time. So Travis asked himself, "If no one invented anything like that yet, WHY NOT ME?" Indeed, why not him? We all know that one person can make a difference, but sometimes we don't realize that that person can be us.

His friend Roger Yates had worked in a small injection molding company and Travis shared his idea. Injection molding is the process of actually producing parts from both plastic and plastic like materials. The process involves heating the core material and injecting it into a cavity where it cools, then hardens and can be sculpted and adjusted to conform to the proper shape. After the product is designed, a mold is made from metal and machined to the proper final dimensions. People in this industry get "pitched" regularly by dreamers wanting to invent or create something and Roger was used to it. A cynic by nature (Travis's words!), Roger loved the idea and referred Travis to a company that could do a prototype and create the molds. The first person that he shared it with declined and did not see the possibilities, but number two did. Tom Freeman was not a musician, but when he told Travis, "I don't even play and I want one!" they both knew there was potential. NOTE: If you ever come up with an idea for something that people WANT, rather than need, you are halfway there. The reality is, most people want to play the guitar more than any other instrument and that desire to play is common in more than 90% of men per the Gallup polls.

All this sounded great, but the reality of that time is that Travis was broke. He lost everything in the Recession and made little teaching guitar. What he had was a dream and hope and respect in the community and some investors with money that saw his passion along with the upside. After a year's time, and over $200,000, they came up with the 17th prototype and **Chord Buddy** was born. His mother, who was ill and had rheumatoid arthritis in her crippled fingers, actually played with that 17th prototype until they manufactured the first finished product a year later. This was more proof that if someone with weakened fingers could use the product, then anyone could, and that was after her not playing for more than 15 years. The one unshakable position that Travis took was that he would not manufacture overseas and wanted to keep it American made, and ideally in his own town. The Alabama economy took a number of hits over the years and storm and tornado damage only made it worse. On top of that there are great risks manufacturing in other countries as Travis told me. "They make two molds, one for you and one for themselves since they know that you won't patent the product in every nation in the world. No inventor wants to have their product stolen, but that's a risk by going overseas."

In October, 2010, the first Chord Buddy was delivered and Travis went into business. His mother was given and played with that very first one in her honor and sadly she passed away just two days later. "Mom gave me the gift of music early in my life and I was able to give it back to her," he shared. Fortunately Travis and company still had investor backing and heavily advertised on TV and local media and had a fantastic Christmas in 2010, selling several hundred thousand of the products. After the first of the year- and most of 2011, it all but vanished. Summer was especially hard since "kids don't play or practice in summer" according to Travis, so even though he started on a high note his attitude and confidence was wavering.

Then, in April, 2011, Travis got THE call, the call that changed his life and the lives of many others. He was called by the ABC hit show Shark Tank, and asked to be a contestant. The show started in August, 2009 with just a few episodes and proved successful and has been on ever since. The panel of "Sharks" are successful entrepreneurs and investors and has consisted of some well know and lesser know- but very wealthy- investors over the years, including Kevin O'Leary, Daymond John, Barbara Corcoran, Kevin Harrington, Robert Herjavec and Mark Cuban. Well known stand up comic Jeff Foxworthy also had his run for a few episodes in Season 2. The panel evaluates and negotiates investment proposals from entrepreneurs/ contestants to take a product to market and each of the sharks grills the "victim" to negotiate the best deal they can. The show started in Canada and was very successful and was later imported into the U.S. and is produced by Mark Burnett, the well known reality show producer that started this "reality show phenomenon" with Survivor in 2000. For any investor wanting to learn how to articulate- succinctly- your business model to a bank, or an investor or a venture capitalist, this is the Super Bowl of pitching, and we're not talking the baseball type. There have been many millionaires created through the show, both in deals struck and even those deals that did not get the Shark's money and especially by the fantastic exposure and publicity generated by the millions of viewers.

When Travis got that fateful call from the show his wife did not even believe him for several days, and it wasn't until the entry package arrived in the mail that she finally did. He was a fan of the show from the very beginning and sent his application in over a year before and totally forgot about it. "I didn't want to get my hopes up," he shared with me, which is understandable since they get thousands of submissions. They taped the show on July 24, 2011 and Travis could do nothing but wait. And hope and pray. And also get ready for what he hoped was a huge spike in demand. "The number I was hoping for was 1000 sales, and I was praying for 3000" he shared. "With 3000 I could pay off all my loans and start making some money again! and I was ready to churn out those kinds of numbers."

The best was yet to come, but so was the worst. Between the time the show taped and when it aired all he could do was wait. And Travis had virtually no money. The electricity was shut off to his home as well as the manufacturing facility the week before the show aired and to keep things going he had to run an extension cord between his place and his neighbors. "It was not a fun Christmas" he confided, "but I had faith." What keeps someone like him and others like him, going? Many would claim him a fool, but I like the expressions "Go big or go home" and "No guts, no glory" since they say it all. There is no back door, no plan B. You have to give up control and get back your life.

The show aired Friday evening on February 3, 2012. Dinah Washington in 1959 had a Grammy winning song called "What a difference a day makes" and she was oh, so right. But even better, what a difference 14 minutes and 32 seconds can make! Following is the transcript of Travis's segment. I am also a fan of the show and have been watching since Day one and saw this live. The exchange between the Sharks and himself was one of the best I have ever seen and kept me on the seat of my chair. I have shortened it just a bit for brevity sake, but if you would like the full transcript, please let us know. Here is the video as it aired: www.abc.go.com/watch/shark-tank/SH559076/VD55167840/week-3, and this is how it went:

The players:
Travis (Perry): contestant
Kevin (O'Leary): estimated worth: from $300M-$3.2B, sold The Learning Company to Mattel Toys
Robert (Herjevec): read on
Mark (Cuban): estimated worth: $2.5B, made it big in tech before the rush, but scored with the sale of Broadcast.com in 1999 for just under $6B
Daymond (John): estimated worth: $100M founder & president of FUBU clothing line
Barbara (Corcoran): estimated worth: $1.5B, real estate tycoon working in the New York market

Introduction from Travis:

Perry: My name is Travis Perry. I am from Dauphin, Alabama, and I have invented a product that allows you to play the guitar instantly.

:   The main reason that people quit is frustration and finger pain. Even Bradi, my eight-year-old daughter, was going to quit guitar and I decided it's high time that somebody did something about it. The area of the country that I live in was hit pretty hard with the economic downturn. One thing that was very important to me was to keep the manufacturing and the jobs in the

U.S. It means a lot to me to give back, so to be able to turn around and offer jobs to people that had lost jobs is as important as the product itself. I really have to get a deal from the sharks because we're at a stage of Chord Buddy — we're like a race car. We've won all the preliminary races, we're on the starting line, and we're running out of gas.

Intro (Perry): My name is Travis Perry. My product is Chord Buddy. I've come to the Shark Tank to ask for $125,000 for a 10% equity stake in my business. My love is music. I have taught thousands of people to play the guitar. Sadly, I've seen thousands quit. The guitar is the most popular instrument in the world but yet it is one of the most frustrating. We all want to play the guitar for one reason. You know what it is — *to meet chicks*! But what if a product existed where you could push a button and play a song and learn the guitar with no frustration? Well, Sharks, there's no "what if." It exists, and it is the award-winning Chord Buddy. There's four buttons. It plays G, D, C, and E_m. With those four chords you can play hundreds of thousands of songs. Y'all, that's done with one button, one finger.

O'Leary: If you were really learning playing by pushing a single button, why are you learning anything?

Perry: Oh, man, the question I was waiting for. It is a cheat, I'll be honest, unless it does this. (Travis pulls a tab from one of the frets of

	the guitar) You pull that out. Now, instead of pressing a button, you're really playing a chord. We have a patented two-month learning system and a DVD that takes you every step of the way from removing your first tab to removing your last one.
Herjevec:	So you slowly take off the different colors?
Perry:	Yeah. Now you're playing what the red one did.
Herjevec:	Where it used to be?
Perry:	Where it used to be.
Cuban:	How much does it cost, Travis?
Perry:	Retail $49.95.
Cuban:	What does it cost to make?
Perry:	Initially, it cost us $9; now we're down to $7.
Cuban:	So if you just want to pick up chicks, it's 50 bucks plus the cost of the guitar.
Perry:	How cheap is that?
Herjevec:	Travis, whenever I drive down the street with my girls and a good guitar riff comes on, I want to be a rock star so bad. If you can teach me how to play the guitar…
Perry:	I promise you I can, right now. Let's do it.
Herjevec:	Let's do it. (Robert leaves the stage and takes the guitar from Travis)
Herjevec:	Okay. Thank you very much. All right. I'll play, you sing.
Perry:	Mash the red one.
Herjevec:	The red one?
Perry:	Uh-huh. *Amazing grace* — green. Just the green, just the green. *How sweet* — back to blue — *the sound…*
Herjevec:	We're jamming, baby.

Perry:	*...that saves a wretch*—Go to red—*like me.* Y'all, what you've just seen him do would take at least two months.
Herjevec:	That's true.
John:	Have you sold any of these?
Perry:	Yes, in one month we did $150,000.
Corcoran:	How?
Perry:	Internet and we set up eight local music stores.
Cuban:	Local where?
Perry:	In L.A., lower Alabama.
Herjevec:	Travis, how did you come up with this?
Perry:	I was teaching my eight-year-old daughter, Bradi, to play a song. She was fixin' to become one of the six out of ten that quit and I said, "Bradi, I've had an idea for 31 years of a magical device and you can press a button and play a song." She looked at me in the eyes and she says, "Daddy, invent that for me." And I did.
Corcoran:	You must be a great dad.
Perry:	(Travis is emotional touched) Thanks. Well, we got through that, didn't we?
O'Leary:	Travis, look, I buy it. You're a great dad, you've very funny too, and maybe you've got something here, but I want to go back to the money because that, in the end that's what it's about, my friend. You're telling me that I can buy 10% of this product—it's not really a company yet—for $125,000, which means I have to look at it and say, "This idea is worth $1.25 million."
Perry:	That's right.
O'Leary:	You walk me through why that's the case, Travis. How much have you done in sales since you started?

Perry:	Since we started; a half a million.
O'Leary:	And you've collected the cash on that?
Perry:	Absolutely.
O'Leary:	You brought in half a million in sales?
Perry:	And I've got P.O.s for another 110 that we're fulfilling now.
John:	Purchase orders?
Perry:	That's right.
O'Leary:	How many do you think you can sell this year, Travis?
Perry:	Well, the only reason I hesitate…
O'Leary:	Don't hesitate.
Perry:	…the largest retail chain in the country is giving us a P.O. in two weeks.
O'Leary:	Have you guestimated what their sell-through is going to be?
Perry:	They've told us 50 per store.
John:	How many doors do they have?
Perry:	They have 5,000 stores.
John:	Who is it?
Perry:	Sam's.
Herjevec:	Wow!
Perry:	Sam's Clubs.
Herjevec:	Wow! Let me ask you this. Why do you need $125,000 today?
Perry:	We're building right now in my plant in Dauphin, Alabama, and, by the way, it's a one hundred percent USA-made product.
Cuban:	Congratulations for that. That's important.
Perry:	Thank you.
O'Leary:	Why aren't you making it in China?
Perry:	I want it to be USA. I think that's the downfall of our country.
O'Leary:	Bet you they can make that for eighty cents.
Perry:	They probably can.
Cuban:	Yeah, you can squeeze another nickel out.

O'Leary:	Not a nickel.
Cuban:	A dollar — sometimes it feels good to do the right thing.
John:	He comes from a territory that's been destroyed; I think the people need the jobs.
Cuban:	Good for you, Travis, good for you.
Perry:	They need 'em bad, they do.
O'Leary:	All right, Travis. I think you have something really interesting here but I don't like your valuation, my friend.
Perry:	Sure.
O'Leary:	But I believe if it works it will get its place in retail in places like Guitar Center. I've lived with guitars my whole life. I got a lot of them. I play guitar. So I'm going to make you an offer. **I'll give you $125,000 for 20% and I'll personally endorse the product, I'll do an infomercial for you, put my face on the box or whatever you want to do, for 12 months.**
Herjevec:	Travis, that's how vain he is; that's how self-important he is. He thinks that his picture on the box is going to sell it.
O'Leary:	Yeah, he does. He does.
Cuban:	Hey, he's big in L.A., lower Alabama.
O'Leary:	Hey, listen, I'm up here for a reason, my friend. Don't make jokes about it.
John:	Travis, sir. I think I'm going to match Voldemort's (**) offer but I think you'll know that I'm a better partner so I'm going to do the same **$125,000 for 20%.**
O'Leary:	This guy cannot play guitar, by the way.
Herjevec:	I think that's the point. Yeah, Barbara, are you in or are you out?
Corcoran:	I'm thinking about it.
Herjevec:	Mark, are you in or are you out?

Cuban:	I'm thinking.
John:	Are you in or are you out?
Herjevec:	Thinking.
Corcoran:	Oh my gosh.
John:	Travis, you have two offers on the table and those offers will soon be gone, so while everybody else is thinking, would you like to make a decision?
Commentator:	**Travis has two offers on the table, but the other three sharks are still in.**
O'Leary:	I'll give you **$125,000 for 20% and I will personally endorse the product.**
John:	I'm going to do the same — **$125,000, 20%**
Herjevec:	Same offer?
Perry:	Endorsement?
John:	I happen to represent a lot of the biggest celebrities in the world.
O'Leary:	But they're not going to get you that for free.
John:	We may work that in.
O'Leary:	You're going to get a free celebrity endorsement?
John:	Absolutely.
Perry:	Wow.
O'Leary:	I don't think so.
Corcoran:	Which celebrity, Daymond?
John:	Don't worry about it.
Corcoran:	I do worry about it because that's swaying him, but I wouldn't promise it without speaking to him.
John:	I can do that because I represent them, so…
Corcoran:	Oh, you're in the agent business!
O'Leary:	You know, the good news is I represent me and I just spoke to myself and I'm okay with it.

Cuban:	I'm vacillating, Travis. I mean I like what you're doing, I love the fact that you're made in the USA but I'm not quite sure that you're going to be able to scale. You're going to have to be that guy that goes on the road show all the time, and how old are your kids now?
Perry:	Ten, three and one.
Cuban:	That's part of the problem, right? That's tough. **So I'm out.**
Corcoran:	I have an offer for you.
Perry:	Okay.
Corcoran:	I'm going to beat this jerk's offer. You don't want to go with him.
O'Leary:	What a witch.
Corcoran:	**I'm going to give you $175,000 for the same 20% with the contingency that $50,000 of that money is used to make an infomercial** and you know why? Because the best thing you have going about you is not just your product, but you, and that's the only missing piece here. You've got to figure a way to take you and multiply it times a thousand, and there's no better medium than television.
O'Leary:	I would not guarantee you're going to be in an infomercial until you've ruled out retail. Don't let an investor tell you how to run your business.
Herjevec:	Travis, infomercials is just another way to sell the product.
Corcoran:	Another way? It puts him in every living room.
Herjevec:	Travis, here's an offer. I'm just a redneck from Croatia like you're a redneck from Alabama. I'll give you the **$125,000 for**

	20%, same offer. I don't think you need more cash; I don't think you need to do the infomercial right now.
Corcoran:	Oh, really? You want to keep him locked up.
Herjevec:	I'll give you $125,000 for 20%. I'm the only one here who wants to be a rock star and can't play, so I'm living up to a promise I made to my daughter…
O'Leary:	Let's summarize what we've got, okay? We've got Croatian rock star wanna-be guy — $125,000 for 20%.
Herjevec:	Am I not the market?
O'Leary:	$125,000 for 20%. We've got "I want to control your life in every way known to man" Barbara.
Corcoran:	Not at all. He's the lead. I just want to help him.
O'Leary:	I'm just pointing out what you do want, and that's $175,000 gets you 20% with her deal but a nightmare from hell to work with, we know that.
Corcoran:	Really?
O'Leary:	I'm a straight shooter here. I just want to give you some money, I love guitar, and if you want my endorsement, you get it for free. And Daymond has some nebulous guy in the sky, we don't know who it is, that maybe will endorse this, but he'll do the same deal–$125,000 for 20%. You're in a really rare spot right now, Travis. Not often in the Shark Tank do you get **four rock solid offers**. Those are pretty good offers.
Corcoran:	Travis, this is a no-brainer. I've offered you $50,000 more to get you to where you need

	to go—to get your personality on TV. People are going to fall in love with you.
O'Leary:	I can get you on TV.
Corcoran:	Look at the offers you're getting. It's your personality that they're falling in love with.
Herjevec:	Look, I'm just a lonely shark here trying to play the guitar, baby.
Perry:	This is so hard. Robert, would you sweeten your offer some way?
Herjevec:	**I'll put the $50,000 aside to produce an infomercial, if we make that decision.**
Perry:	So it's $125,000 cash with $50,000 in escrow for an infomercial?
Herjevec:	Absolutely, because I'm going to quit this shark thing, baby. I'm going to go on the road.
Perry:	Me and you, me and you.
Herjevec:	I'm going to become a rock star.
Perry:	I'm talking about duo in the Redneck Riviera.
Herjevec:	Me, too, baby. Do we have a deal, do we have a deal? Travis?
Perry:	Robert, the deal is with you.
Corcoran:	Damn!
Herjevec:	I'm gonna be a rock star.
Corcoran:	I can't watch.

Herjevec:	*Well, Travis and I, we did ourselves a damn deal.*
Perry:	*We got a deal in the Tank and we're gonna make millions.*
Herjevec:	***Million!***
Perry:	My family now will be financially stable. This is a life-changing moment for me.

** (Harry Potter movie villain)

Notes & Lessons:
Travis did everything 100% right. He showed his commitment, his focus, *passion* and his *drive*; had a great *story, emotional connection* due to his desire to keep jobs in Alabama and especially created a *personal connection* to the Sharks- especially Robert- who wanted to play the guitar and was willing to partner with Travis to do that and make a lot of money at the same time. He used humor and had fun with them.

On Thursday, February 2, 2012, the day before the show, Travis sold four Chord Buddies. He was praying for 3000 sales from the show and when I interviewed him 12 days after the show aired they had sold *7000 over the following two days* and that number was growing every day. They are manufacturing 24 hours a day and in less than 2 weeks they hired 11 new people with more due to come on board. I asked if he was ready for this Overnight Success and to manufacture the required volume, and he said "I thought I was", but truly this is beyond his dreams. Travis is proving something that I have said for years and that is our economic turnaround cannot be mandated and it will not come by legislation. It will come from people like Travis with a dream and idea. He was fortunate that destiny or providence or whatever you want to call it smiled on him, but the credit really belongs to him. It was his idea, and even though many of us have (or had) great ideas, Travis ACTED ON IT. One small company can become a private economic development force in a small town that has had its share of challenges with the economy and the tornado carnage experienced in 2011.

I asked about projections for the year and he said it was a moving target, but thought $1 million in sales just from the Tank is realistic and they are working on another deal- even larger- that could multiply that to more than $6 million for the year. Travis retained a 51% controlling interest and there are outstanding shares available should they need to bring in more capital. Robert Herjavec is now his partner and good friend and I will assume he is happy with the deal since it will make him lots of money, too. For $125,000, and a promise of $50K more for a television infomercial (which they may not need), he was able to purchase 20% of a potentially multi-million dollar company, create a wonderful economic impact on a hard hit part of the company, and to top it all off, he learned how to play the guitar for his daughters! Even though Dad was a millionaire several times over he wanted to be his families Rock Star and teach them how to play. You can be sure he is their Canadian Idol for sure.

Robert is a wonderful mentor and even though both he and Travis are Boomers it shows the great value of partnering and collaboration. All the Sharks wanted in, but one of the biggest deciding factors was Robert's sincere passion to play the guitar. If you look at the video clip you'll see Travis give the guitar to Robert to demonstrate and even though others wanted to try, Robert would not let it go! The Yugoslavian (now Croatia) born Robert is 48 and made his millions with BRAK systems which he started in 1990 and later became the largest provider of Internet Security Software in Canada, which is where he now resides, and in the most affluent community in the entire country. BRAK was sold in 2000 to AT&T for $100M and he took a position with RAMP Networks as Vice President and RAMP later was sold to Nokia for $225K. Robert knows how to find the money and is an active venture capitalist along with founding The Herjavec Group which is, what else?, an Internet security company.

Mark Cuban, the billionaire owner of the Dallas Mavericks (net worth $2.5 billion) was interested, but passed and actually told Travis that he didn't NEED the Sharks; all he needed was the exposure of the show- and he got it. I asked Travis how he was able to absorb all this and understand the finances involved and he shared a bit more of his past: "Dad was a very successful businessman and owned several and I majored in finance in college and minored in PR. This is a great chance to take those theories I learned and actually use them!"

They are also working on a prototype for other stringed instruments, like banjo and mandolin, but they will not come about until the Chord Buddy for the guitar is purring along. "The markets for them are much, much smaller, but as a music lover I feel that we should help them, too."
Can dreams come true? Was Travis "lucky?" Sure he was lucky, it is part of the process, but the chances of you winning a million dollar lottery is not a future you can plan or depend on. It is random and it is difficult to capture lightning in a bottle. You need a dream and you need tenacity to reach your goals. The saying, "The harder I work, the luckier I get," has truth beneath the surface.

UPDATE: The day before going to print with this book I called Travis for an update. For the months of February to mid-March:
- They sold 15,000 unites
- Created a QVC video
- And hired 25 new employees

To reach Travis: (www.chordbuddy.com)

DON'T CONFUSE YOUR PATH
WITH YOUR DESTINATION.
JUST BECAUSE IT'S STORMY
NOW DOESN'T MEAN YOU
AREN'T HEADED FOR
SUNSHINE.

Unknown

(30) The Tide rushes in- again

The Baby Boomers were the first generation that created by shear size a large groundswell so big that they actually gave it a name: The Baby Boomer Movement. They were the first generation raised on television, and created many milestones of the past 50 years, including the Love movement of the sixties, the "Me" decade and the free-love (sex) movement of the seventies, and were the first to take technology from large corporate mainframes of the past to our desks and now into Smart Phones that we carry in our pockets. They are a generation whose time had come... and gone. At least that is what many of them feel. With their best days behind them, the Boomers want to live forever, live free and stay healthy and remain a force in society. Unfortunately some may feel that their best days are behind them and the legacy remains what it is-or was. **I disagree**. You can learn many things quickly and master some, but there is one thing that takes time: experience. It cannot be rushed; it can only be absorbed, massaged, and adjusted to new beginnings. There is a difference between knowledge and wisdom and many Boomers have both.

The national and world economies are in the tank and things will never be the way they used to be. You can discard all rule books that are more than five years old and from now on write them on erasable boards since they will never have much longevity any more. Change is not change for change sake; it is change for the duration of time. America remains an economic power, but not a Super Power as before, and what used to be a commanding lead and presence is fragile and will be usurped by Far Eastern powers. What we have in surplus is ingenuity and drive and the memories of what came before us, so rather than fighting the World Flattening Phenomenon, let's marshal our resources and talents and build a new machine, maybe smaller and less powerful, but still a force to be reckoned with.

The Boomers have some unique offerings that no other generation or *country* can compete with: 40 years of experience of being knocked down, getting up and doing it again. No other nation can bring the power of 73 million voices of experience and combine them with 80 million voices of a new generation: The Millennials.

So imagine this: You take the collective grit and determination of the Boomers, the experience of being raised in a harder world with less toddling, less technology, but more of a fighter instinct. Now add in the Millennials that are lacking some of those things, but are quick on their feet, quick in their minds, can multi-task all day (and night) long, and know how to take something-*anything*- and share it with thousands or tens of thousands of people with a few key strokes. So what is their message? How do they use this power at their fingertips? "With great power comes great responsibility," said Uncle Ben in the "Spiderman" movie and he is right. These Gen Ys that may think they will stay young forever (hell, we did and look where we are now?) have a deep responsibility. It is up to them to bring America back to Economic Equality if not more. And I believe they can do that, with nurturing and guidance, mentorship and someone to support and encourage them. I call this **The New Economic Paradigm**, and I believe it is an attainable and worthwhile cause.

I start many business books and finish few. I find them high in theory and concept but low in practicality and like many of you, we all have good intentions, but questionable execution. Likewise I find great solace in inspirational books and morality tales and they make us "feel good" and *want* to change, but how often do we? And also, like many of you, I have been to countless workshops and seminars all designed to change our lives and make us smart and make us money, but the results rarely follow the effort spent in hearing someone preach- or sell. Nothing is better than reading a book or going to a weekend workshop and coming out pumped up and ready to change and to take on new challenges, but historically few execute. In years past I have known many promoters personally and many pitchmen; some good, and some very, very bad. The "back of the room" rush to buy crap mentality can take hold with the feelings just experienced, but the majority of kits and training programs that are sold on site- are never even opened. Some are read; few are acted upon. I hope to break that cycle. If you have read this far I hope you understand the mission-our mission-and that is to become a catalyst for change and for improvement. YOUR improvement- and the improvement of others. The only way to do that is to take action and that will be in the form of classes- on-going classes- that brings together the experience and insight of the Boomers and the drive, energy, and tech savviness of the Millennials. The **Mentor2Mentor program** will be the next steps available which will include on-going trainings held nationwide and taught with a very specific curriculum designed to take the powers of both generations and to formulate a *Two-Year Plan for Success*.

This book may inspire you to create your own Two-Year Success Plan and nothing would please me more! Regardless of which "generation" you are in, success is within your reach. But heed these words: *it is easy to fail alone, but it is difficult to succeed alone.*

This is Part I of the next step which I call Baby Boomers: *Rebooted*. They (we) may be older (not old) but we are not dead yet! If any generation can reinvent itself it's the savvy Baby Boomers! You interested? And this is a multi-generational offering opportunity, so all ages, colors, ethnicities and religions are welcome!

There is a great cartoon I once read that shows two vultures sitting on a telephone line, waiting for road kill; something to eat. Vultures are carrion eaters, they wait for something to be killed and eat what remains, but one vulture said to the other one, "Patience my ass! I'm going to kill something." So the question is, are you going to starve to death and lament over what never was, or was before, or are you going to create what is meant to be?

"THERE IS NO GREATER AGONY THAN BEARING AN UNTOLD STORY INSIDE YOU."
- MAYA ANGELOU

(31) Conclusion?/ Epilogue: ep·i·logue also
ep·i·log (ĕp'ə-lôg', -lŏg') ☒
n. a conclusion or commentary on what has occurred or come before

In 1982 I was in my second year as a real estate agent, I was 27 years old and I got a quick lesson in entrepreneurship. We didn't use that word much back then; it was just called "being self-employed." As wonderful as it is having no boss (a fallacy), it also offered no security. You learn by your mistakes as always and with 1981 being my first full year I got a quick education in tax planning. Or lack of tax planning. I had no idea I had to pay tax on that small amount of money I made the year before, so I had not budgeted or planned and got hit with a tax I was not ready for. The early years in the world of self-employment were challenging for me as it was and is for anyone that has lived that life. One day I was complaining (whining?) to one of my fellow agents about my woes and he gave me a small legal sized poster with the words "Don't Quit" on the top. He had pinned it to the wall in our lunch room and he made me a copy. I read the words and had the original document on my wall until just a few years ago when I finally had to discard it because it was tattered and faded. I copied the words and created a brand new version for myself and I now share it with you. Since 1982 these words have been close to me, not always within sight, but always within reach. And I have had to reach for them many, many times over a 30 year span and every time I do I stop feeling sorry for myself and accept what *is*, and change what **isn't**.

Don't Quit

When things go bad as they sometimes will,
When the road you're trudging seems all uphill,
When the funds are low and the debts are high,
And you want to smile, but you have to sigh,
When the care is pressing you down a bit-
Rest if you must, but don't you quit.

Life is queer with its twists and turns,
As every one of us sometimes learns,
And many a person turns about
When they might have won had they stuck it out.
Don't give up though the pace seems slow-
You may succeed with another blow.
Often the struggler has given up
When he might have captured the victor's cup;
And he learned too late
When the night came down,
How close he was to the golden crown.

Success is failure turned inside out-
So stick to the fight when you're hardest hit,-
It's when things seem worst that you mustn't quit.

I have no idea who authored this prose, but it has saved me many anguishing moments that might have lingered a bit longer had I not had that reality check. As significant as these words are to me, I invite you to integrate them into *your* psyche, too. If ever you feel you can't take it any more, or you're up to **HERE** with challenges, please pull these words out and repeat them to yourself a time or three. I avoided many wasted hours of despondency and I think it can work for you, too, but hope you never need to find out.

Poets and songwriters share their thoughts about time, like the pragmatic Mick Jagger and the Rolling Stones who say that "Time waits for no man and it won't wait for me" and John Lennon philosophically shares that life is what happens when you're busy making other plans. Both are true and one of those singers is now 68 years old and the other passed long, long before his time should gave come. Time is arbitrary and it's also quite specific and scientists have broken down seconds into millions of bite sized pieces, as much as a billionth of a second, called a nanosecond, yet until civilization "invented" and required time, we measured by the moon and the sun and the seasons. One of my business partners was born in Kenya, in the bush, just like a Hollywood version of a Kenyan Bushman. He does not know his date of birth since it was not important in his culture. All that mattered was that the child was healthy, so the date was unknown, as was the weight and other dimensions. He never thought about a birth day and had to make one up when he came to the United States.

To quote another song man, Bob Dylan told us in 1964 "The Times they are a-changin'" and that is just as true today, and the Fifth Dimension shared that we are in the "Age of Aquarius." Are we? Astrologically speaking we should be in a period of enlightenment and hope, and even though that song was from 1966 I propose that we keep that same attitude. We can be in that period of enlightenment and hope if we choose to be and we make it so.

On a ponderous note I will leave you with this thought. The End of the World is coming. No really, the Mayans predicted it will end on December 21, 2012, so we need to move quickly. I had an interesting conversation with my cousin Michael and he has a theory that the world really is ending, but not in a physical sense, but in a philosophical one. We're tired of hearing the same old rhetoric from politicians and leaders- regardless of party- that talk a good game, but do nothing effective. Rules; laws; changed tax guidelines, they really don't impact the mindset of the average American. So I propose that we- you, me and others- regardless of whether we are Boomers or Gen X, Y or Z, start making a difference on our own. Michael says he is not an optimist, nor a pessimist, but is a Realist, which means he tempers his conclusions with experience and thought. I like that concept and propose we do the same thing.

Take control of your life. If you absolutely must go out and get a job, then do so, but for most of you reading this, that is not our focus. We do not want to be working at Wal-mart as a greeter when we retire- unless we are independently wealthy and doing it for fun! For Boomers, going back to school is probably not in the cards, unless you are taking specific and specialized courses. But getting a degree with the intention of becoming a butcher, baker or candlestick maker is probably not the best use of your time.

Per Challenger, Gray and Christmas consulting, in 2011 just 3.3% of Americans started their own business, down from 4.7% in 2010. Compare that to 1989 when over 20% started a business and until 1997 the numbers were usually double digit. So what happened? Lack of money? Lack of hope? Fear? Maybe a combination of all of them. So for you Boomers out there our best years are *not* behind us, but are yet to be experienced.

Be the Best you can be and make yourself as Successful as you want.

To leave you with a smile, I present a comic from Joe Morgan, age 66, most certainly a Baby Boomer, but not an overnight success. Joe has been creating his offbeat humor since 1979 and provides comic relief for not just one strip, but for three, including this one from "Willy n' Ethel." He has published over 22,000 strips over the past thirty plus years and has been proclaimed by Guinness World Records as the most prolific cartoonist in the world. I doubt he will ever stop and *neither should you*! This one caught my eye, Joe was gracious enough to allow it to be included in the Baby Boomer's Guide, so heed his words and don't just go out and try, but go out and do.

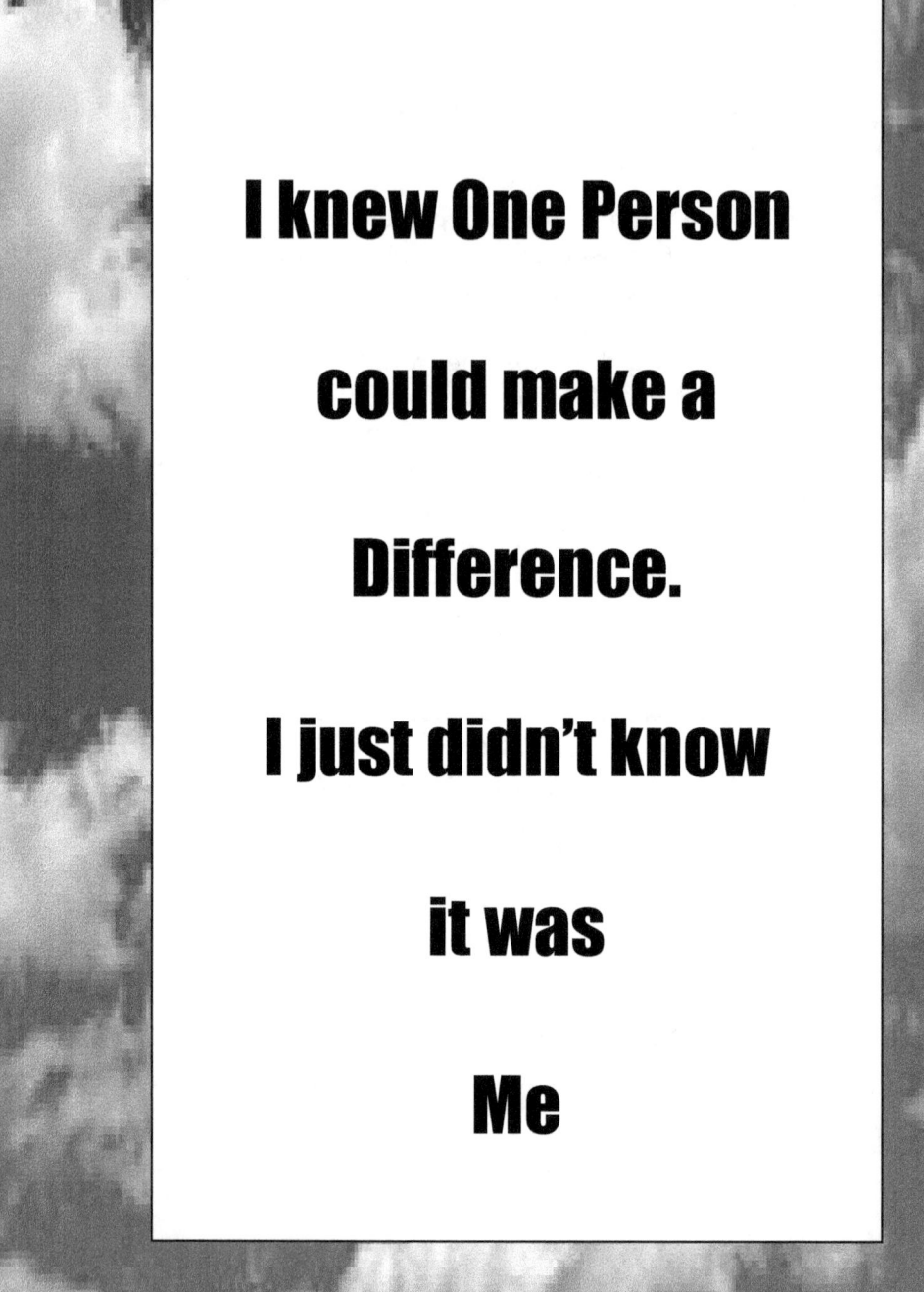

I knew One Person

could make a

Difference.

I just didn't know

it was

Me

This book is not about concepts, but about motivating you to move forward in the direction you wish to go. Talk is cheap without a plan behind it, so this is the final step. I have read many books that offer charts and want you to make long lists of different exercises and such, but the longer the list the greater the chance you will lose focus and not get *anything* done. So the steps are few:

1. Assess your current business if you have one and ask yourself "Is it really what I want to do and I am really good at it?" It may be that you really just need a minor course correction, not a brand new ship. If that is the case we can offer you some worksheets via e-mail that will allow you to complete an honest self-evaluation and move in that right direction. The web site is www.BoomersSuccessGuide.com and we ask that you *follow our blog* and updates on the wonderful stories that *have not* been heard yet. Maybe one of those stories is *yours*?? We will offer a *free introductory recorded call* as this movement gains momentum, so check in frequently.

2. If you don't have a business, but would like to start one, then go back to the chart on page 132 where I analyzed my own strengths and weaknesses. I suggest you share this list with someone that knows you to gain their insight to see if it gels with yours. It may, but possibly not.

3. Now it's time to put the two bookends together, the Boomers and the Millennials. Boomers Success Guide will organize local groups to bring the creative minds together- of all ages- and develop internal business relationships. The reason the group is called **mentor2mentor** is because it is a

two way street and neither side is better or more significant than the other. I have been a fan of incubation centers for years, but have found them too narrowly focused on high tech or bio tech and companies that may be candidates for massive potential or going "public." I think that is great, but that may be more than you want or wish to commit too. I believe that incubators can be evolutionary- and revolutionary- for any and every type business- including yours. Visit our web site: www.mentor2mentor.com to stay on top of new chapters forming and opportunities available. If you wish to be a Team Leader, please let us know. Think outside the box and also outside your local area. We welcome you to a brand new you.

"Only those who dare to fail greatly can ever achieve greatly."

Those words were spoken by the late Senator Robert F. Kennedy, who even in such a ridiculously short time on earth made a difference and created an impact. So what can you do with double the amount of time that RFK was alive since he was here for just 42 years??

For one thing, don't fail. "Success is a state of mind; failure is only temporary." That is my quote and feel free to share it at will. Keep these thoughts in mind:

- Never see failure as failure; never see rejection as rejection. These are opportunities for you to grow
- Never see failure as failure; It is feedback to change course to a new direction
- Never see failure as failure; it is a chance to develop a sense of humor
- Never see failure as failure; it is a chance to correct the process and practice to perfection

- Never see failure as failure; it is the game you must play to win

Those words were shared with me by a brilliant trainer in one of the few "J-O-B-S" I have had. He also said: "I am not judged by the number of time I fail, but by the number of times I succeed, which is in direct proportion to the numbers of times I try and fail, but keep trying," so take these thoughts to heart.

As I was finishing up the final words in my story I got a note from a LinkedIn (a social media site) connection in South Africa of all places. As we must understand, the world truly IS flat and doing business with someone that is 10,500 miles away (thank you, Internet) and someone down the street is not much different. She asked me what was my motivation to write this book? You all know the longer, more detailed version, but I tried to encapsulate it in just a few sentences and this is what I told her:

What finally triggered me to write the story that has been in my mind for three years took me 90 days to finish and 30 years of experience to tap in to was fear- and pain. As I was at my lowest point emotionally and financially I had ever been in, I was at risk of losing my house, my wife and my family and with my stress level off the chart I thought I was going to die. No exaggeration. The legacy that I had at that time was less than impressive so I decided I would share my story and search out the stories of others and tell the world that you may lose confidence, but never lose hope.

The Guide tells my less than impressive tale of failure after failure, yet continuing to get up and try again. I felt I was in the 9th round of a 10 round fight and wasn't sure if I could do it again. A gentlemen I knew very casually changed the course of my destiny when I shared my idea, he loved my concept and told me I could do it. I had lost confidence in myself as had many others, but this man objectively knew that I had the spark in me and just needed to create an inferno and that is what happened. The book has saved my life and that is not just a statement, but my entire mental state and optimism for the future is as high as it's ever been. The thought of traveling and having fun and seeing the world I thought was a long-gone dream. But you never know, I may end up speaking in South Africa!

For the past several years I have been operating at less than peak efficiency and now I feel I am over 90%. As I take the stage and create evolutionary mentorship programs for Boomers and Gen Ys my attitude will go higher still. You see I still don't know if anyone will like my words since it's hard to be objective with our own thoughts. I know in MY heart I will do whatever is necessary to create as much positive impact as possible, regardless of book sales.

For years I tried to control everything in my life and it brought misery and failure, so I am now letting go and controlling just me and my efforts.

For several years I have been involved with Peer to Peer and mentorship classes and recently one of our students asked a question that business owners ask all the time. He is in the insurance business and always talks about what he "should do" and "could do", but he never does. So when he asked the question of "How do you finally get to the point where you take action?" I responded as follows: "You take action when you reach a point where you cannot take the pain any more. When you are so scared that you will be like this always, you finally break through. When you are tired of making excuses and looking at yourself as a failure, that is when you change your life."

He tapped into my inner soul with that question and I hope I have likewise done with you. I cannot wait to hear of your successes regardless of the Generational box you fit within. It's all about "Creating businesses; creating jobs, maintaining hope..."

Do you have a story to share? Can you inspire others to keep on trying and overcome any kind of adversity? There are many more untold stories, so we welcome yours.

Norm Bour is a highly unemployable, lifelong entrepreneur. Even as a young man, before the word "entrepreneur" was commonplace, Norm was a restless soul, always looking for "more." After thirty years of trying and failing and getting up again, Norm finally found his calling after many decades, and that is to inspire people with hope and offer guidance on how to find their calling. The roads through the worlds of real estate and securities and mortgages and radio offered the background to do what he likes most; teach business people how to adapt and reinvent- and to succeed. He had to learn some hard lessons himself so others could avoid those pains and suffering.

This book has allowed him to give up control of things that are uncontrollable and to regain a Life.

Future books are in the planning and conception stages including a sequel to this Guide and several others along the same mind set.

(34) References

TIME magazine: Gen-X: The Ignored Generation?, April 16, 2008
www.time.com/time/arts/article/0,8599,1731528,00.html

USA Today: Generation Y: They've arrived at work with a new attitude, November 6, 2005
www.usatoday.com/money/workplace/2005-11-06-gen-y_x.htm

Society for Human Resource Management: Mixing it up
www.weknownext.com/workforce/mixing-it-up

Success.com: Success at Any Age
www.successmagazine.com/Success-at-Any-Age/PARAMS/article/384/channel/20

Invest.com: How big is E-commerce industry?
www.invesp.com/blog/ecommerce/how-big-is-ecommerce-industry.html

How many are there.net: How Many Social Networking Websites Are There?, August 11, 2011
www.howmanyarethere.net/how-many-social-networking-websites-are-there/

Top 15 Most Popular Web 2.0 Websites, February 2012
www.ebizmba.com/articles/web-2.0-websites

Facebook Statistics by country
www.socialbakers.com/facebook-statistics/

Onlinecollege.org, 50 Famously Successful People Who Failed At First
www.onlinecollege.org/2010/02/16/50-famously-successful-people-who-failed-at-first/

DrShannonreese.com, The Truth Behind 22+ "Overnight Success" Stories
blog.drshannonreece.com/2011/04/18/the-truth-behind-22-overnight-success-stories/

The 1970's Pet Rocks Craze
www.petarock.homestead.com/1970craze.html
www,minyanville: Crazy Business Ideas That Actually Worked
www.minyanville.com/special-features/articles/pet-rock-gary-dahl-joke-pet/7/17/2010/id/29179

www.ingramcontent.com/pod-product-compliance
Lightning Source LLC
Chambersburg PA
CBHW051457170526
45166CB00001B/276